100 Algebra Workouts
and Practical Teaching Tips

An Essential Tool for Today's Middle School Mathematics Teachers

Based on Middle School Math Standards and Curricula

Written by Tony G. Williams, Ed.D.

Illustrated by Corbin Hillam

Teaching & Learning Company
1204 Buchanan St., P.O. Box 10
Carthage, IL 62321-0010

This book belongs to

_____

Dedications

Dedicated to my parents,
Jean and Grady,
who are retired math teachers;
and to my wife, Sharon;
and our triplets—TLC
(Tony, Leah and Christina).

Cover design by Sara King.

Copyright © 2008, Teaching & Learning Company

ISBN 13: 978-1-57310-559-0

Printing No. 987654321

Teaching & Learning Company
1204 Buchanan St., P.O. Box 10
Carthage, IL 62321-0010

At the time of publication, every effort was made to insure the accuracy of the information included in this book. However, we cannot guarantee that the agencies and organizations mentioned will continue to operate or to maintain these current locations.

Dear Teacher or Parent,

Algebra provides unique opportunities for all students, while opening academic doors for those with diverse backgrounds and varying overall abilities. Research shows that algebra is the gateway to success for most students. There is a positive correlation between completing algebra and being college bound, highly employable, enrolled in higher math and science courses and confident in higher learning. In this book, you will find the most comprehensive collection of algebra workout activities and practical teaching tips for today's middle and high school teachers of algebra. In an age where teachers must compete for their students' attention against a number of influences (Internet, television, video games, peer pressure and other social factors), it is even more critical to develop algebra lessons that capture students' interest, promote and enhance the desire for learning, and reinforce algebraic skills. This resource book includes 100 sensational algebra workouts designed specifically to engage students' exploration of algebra by providing fun, thought-provoking, interesting, skill-building, algebra-related activities. Students will see that algebra can be fun and exciting.

The workout process is a vital part of any algebra lesson. It should be an inviting, settling and stimulating process that readies students for that day's lesson. The best way to start an algebra lesson is with a workout that engages students with algebra. This resource book can help turn on the "light" within students and foster their curiosity for algebra. Not only are these workouts fun, they are based on standard middle school and high school algebra curricula. Each workout is presented on a ready-to-use, blackline master. Each workout also includes a solution key or mini-lesson with background, discussion, strategy and demonstration for solving each problem. These workouts can be easily copied onto transparencies for full class instruction and discussion.

At the end of the book are 14 practical teaching tips for today's classroom. These practical techniques and strategies specifically address the current demands and challenges facing today's algebra teachers, particularly in large urban school settings. The tips cover a broad spectrum of critical areas, ranging from classroom management to online grade books to graphing calculators. This book also includes suggestions for the use of the workouts and weekly workout sheets that can be used to track the workout.

I hope you find these workouts useful as you introduce your students to the exciting world of algebra and the opportunities that await them.

Sincerely,

Tony

Tony G. Williams, Ed.D.

TABLE OF CONTENTS

TLC10559 Copyright © Teaching & Learning Company, Carthage, IL 62321-0010

Activity Suggestions

Introduction

In this resource book, you will find 100 algebra workouts that support your algebra curricula. Each workout was designed as a student activity and class discussion for the first three to ten minutes of class. The workouts cover a thorough and broad range of algebraic concepts, from linear equations to factoring to pure fun. The workouts are presented in 13 units:

1. Foundation
2. Equations
3. Games, Fun and Mystery
4. Linear Equations
5. System of Equations
6. Polynomials
7. Factual, Exploratory and Logic
8. Factoring
9. Pre-Geometry
10. Radicals
11. PSAT Prep
12. Quadratic Equations
13. Teaching Tips

Teachers know that workouts are an effective tool in teaching algebra. Workouts also allow teachers a few valuable minutes for administrative duties (attendance, announcements, etc.) while settling students for the upcoming lesson. Here are some suggestions to help you get the most of the workouts in this book.

The Daily Workouts Sheet and Sequence

The workouts in this book may be used with the Daily Workout sheets on page 8 and on the inside back cover of this book (or with similar forms developed by the teacher). The Daily Workout sheets can be used for 10-12 workouts.

One workout sheet includes spaces for specific days of the week along with one graph, and the other workout sheet is for more general use and includes two graphs and a PSAT grid.

Many of the workout activities can be used with related or unrelated lesson materials, while most follow in sequence the standard Algebra I curriculum. When selecting a workout to be used with unrelated lesson material, you are encouraged to skip around and use the activity that best suits the need for the day. For workouts used with related lesson material, you'll find the sequence useful in accompanying core algebraic standards.

Using the Workouts

Each day's workout should be projected on the overhead screen as students enter the classroom. Once seated, students should immediately begin the activity. You can read or assign a student to read the activity to assist students whose view is obstructed or who are visually impaired. If it is a more complex workout, you should also explain the activity in more detail. The workout activities in this book are designed to last from three to ten minutes. During this time, walk around the classroom to make sure all students are on task and understand the activity. You can also use this to take attendance, check homework, return/collect papers, make announcements or do other administrative tasks.

At the end of the workout, initiate a discussion about the solution. Ask for volunteers or call on students for responses. Allow two to three additional minutes for related discussion and questions. You could also use an overhead transparency of the solution key to generate discussion.

TLC10559 Copyright © Teaching & Learning Company, Carthage, IL 62321-0010

Grading Workouts

It is important that the workouts are incorporated into students' grades so students recognize their value. It is recommended that the workouts be worth 5% to 10% of the each student's grade. The workout sheets should be collected and evaluated by the teacher on a periodic basis. Workouts should be graded primarily on the effort of students. Because the workouts serve to reinforce skills, introduce new ideas and explore the fun applications of algebra, the effort should outweigh correctness of response.

Periodically, perhaps once each grading period, students should be given an opportunity to research/develop their own algebra workouts for a grade or extra credit. Students can be quite resourceful and creative in developing workout activities. The workouts should be a problem, drill or activity that is fascinating, thought-provoking and utilizes algebra. Display some of your students' best algebra workouts on the overhead projector screen and save them for future use.

Workout Responses

There are several types of workout activities presented in this book, including 1. computational, 2. problem solving, 3. choice (multiple choice, fact or fiction, or matching), 4. graphs and 5. group activities. For computational, problem solving and graph workouts, encourage students to show as much work as possible on the workout sheet. Evaluate this type of workout based on work shown by the student.

Some workouts will give students a choice (multiple choice, fact or fiction, or matching) for the response. Encourage students to express on their answer sheets (and orally during the discussion) their reasoning for making a particular choice. In evaluating these workout responses, look for clarity of expression as well as logic and creativity. For workouts with group activities, evaluate students on their effort, cooperativeness and teamwork.

Finally, there are workouts that require students to use logic and reasoning to draw conclusions. In addition to algebraic skills, good reading and writing skills are essential for students' success. These workouts will provide an excellent opportunity for teachers to further develop students' reading, writing and communication skills. Encourage students to express (orally and/or in writing) the reasoning or logic behind their decisions.

Workout for Success

Algebra is the gateway to success for many students, and the workout process is a vital part of any algebra lesson. It should be an inviting, stimulating process that readies students for that day's lesson. There is no better way to start an algebra lesson than with a workout that excites students about algebra.

Daily Workouts

Student: _____ Period: _____

Teacher: _____

Week of _____ – _____   Week of _____ – _____

Score/Grade _____   Score/Grade _____

Monday _____ Activity: _____ Answer:	Tuesday _____ Activity: _____ Answer:
Wednesday _____ Activity: _____ Answer:	
Thursday _____ Activity: _____ Answer:	Friday _____ Activity: _____ Answer:
	Day/Date: _____ Activity: _____ Answer: _____

8

Bingo!

B	I	N	G	O
25	-12	-34	15	-4
-9	-14	3	-11	-7
14	8	FREE	10	11
30	7	-12	-15	-8
4	-32	9	31	-25

Directions: Copy the BINGO table and cross out any squares whose number appears as the answer to one of the problems below. If you get 5 in a row, you've got "BINGO!"

1. $-20 + (-14) =$ ____
2. $-8 + 17 =$ ____
3. $-16 + 9 =$ ____
4. $19 + (-8) =$ ____
5. $11 - (-20) =$ ____

6. $8 - 20 =$ ____
7. $-18 - (-4) =$ ____
8. $-11 - 14 =$ ____
9. $4(-8) =$ ____
10. $(-5)(-3) =$ ____

11. $(-2)^3 =$ ____
12. $(-2)(5)(-1) =$ ____
13. $\frac{36}{-3} =$ ____
14. $-18 \div -6 =$ ____
15. $\frac{-24}{6} =$ ____

Absolute Value

Absolute value is the unit value a number is from zero on the number line. The symbol for absolute value is two vertical lines (| |). Examples: |6| = 6 and |-6| = 6. Note that the absolute value of any number is always greater than or equal to zero. Evaluate the following expressions:

a. $|-9|$

b. $|\frac{7}{8}|$

c. $|-9| + |12|$

d. $|3 - 5|$

e. $|-11| - (-11)$

Solution #1

The shaded block is the winner. All of you should be winners!

B	I	N	G	O
25	-12	-34	15	-4
-9	-14	3	-11	-7
14	8	FREE	10	11
30	7	-12	-15	-8
4	-32	9	31	-25

1. $-20 + (-14) = -34$
2. $-8 + 17 = 9$
3. $-16 + 9 = -7$
4. $19 + (-8) = 11$
5. $11 - (-20) = 31$

6. $8 - 20 = -12$
7. $-18 - (-4) = -14$
8. $-11 - 14 = -25$
9. $4(-8) = -32$
10. $(-5)(-3) = 15$

11. $(-2)^3 = -8$
12. $(-2)(5)(-1) = 10$
13. $\frac{36}{-3} = -12$
14. $-18 \div -6 = 3$
15. $\frac{-24}{6} = -4$

Solution #2

The answers are:

a. $|-9| = 9$

b. $|\frac{7}{8}| = \frac{7}{8}$

c. $|-9| + |12| = 9 + 12 = 21$

d. $|3 - 5| = |-2| = 2$

e. $|-11| - (-11) = 11 - (-11) = 22$

10

Collecting Like Terms

Workout #3

Like terms have the same variable(s) and exponent(s). The terms 2xy and xy are like terms, but x^2 and x^3 are not. Like terms may be collected by adding or subtracting the coefficients in front of those terms. For example, $4x - 2x + x = 3x$.

Simplify:

1. $2x + y - x + 3y$

2. $xy - 3xy$

3. $5x + 4y - 2x^2 - xy$

4. $-5x - y - 3x + 2y$

5. $-6z^2 - 3 - z^2 + 7$

Signs and Symbols

Workout #4

Match the sign or symbol with its meaning.

a. $|...|$ b. π c. $\pm$ d. $\leq$

e. $\approx$ f. $\neq$ g. $>$ h. $\sqrt{}$

_____ 1. plus or minus

_____ 2. square root

_____ 3. absolute value

_____ 4. 3.14

_____ 5. approximately

_____ 6. less than or equal to

_____ 7. not equal to

_____ 8. greater than

Solution #3

The answers are:

1. $2x + y - x + 3y =$ **$x + 4y$**

2. $xy - 3xy =$ **$-2xy$**

3. $5x + 4y - 2x^2 - xy =$ **already simplified**

4. $-5x - y - 3x + 2y =$ **$-8x + y$**

5. $-6z^2 - 3 - z^2 + 7 =$ **$-7z^2 + 4$**

Solution #4

The answers are:

c. $\pm$	1. plus or minus	
h. $\sqrt{}$	2. square root	
a. $|...|$	3. absolute value	
b. π	4. 3.14 pi	
e. $\approx$	5. approximately	
d. $\leq$	6. less than or equal to	
f. $\neq$	7. not equal to	
g. $>$	8. greater than	

Multiplying Terms with Exponents

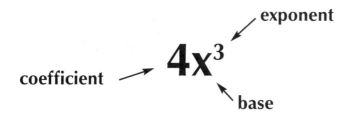

exponent

coefficient

$4x^3$

base

When multiplying terms with exponents, you multiply the coefficients and add the exponents of the like bases (same variable). For example,
$3x^2 \cdot 4x^3 = (3 \cdot 4) \, x^{(2 + 3)} = 12x^5$

Multiply:

a. $x^2 \cdot 3x$

b. $-4x^3 \cdot -3x^5$

c. $(2xy^3)(5x^3y^4)$

d. $(x^2)(2y^3)(-xy)$

Power to a Power

When you raise a term with an exponent to a power, raise the coefficient to the power and multiply the exponent by the power. For example, $(2x^3)^3 = 2^3x^{3 \cdot 3} = 8x^9$.

Simplify:

a. $(x^2)^4$

b. $(3x^4)^3$

c. $(4xy^2)^2$

d. $(-2x^3y^5)^5$

e. $(5x^4y^2)^0$

Solution #5

The answers are:

a. $x^2 \cdot 3x = \mathbf{3x^3}$

b. $-4x^3 \cdot -3x^5 = \mathbf{12x^8}$

c. $(2xy^3)(5x^3y^4) = \mathbf{10x^4y^7}$

d. $(x^2)(2y^3)(-xy) = \mathbf{-2x^3y^4}$

Solution #6

The answers are:

a. $(x^2)^4 = \mathbf{x^8}$

b. $(3x^4)^3 = \mathbf{27x^{12}}$

c. $(4xy^2)^2 = \mathbf{16x^2y^4}$

d. $(-2x^3y^5)^5 = \mathbf{-32x^{15}y^{25}}$

e. $(5x^4y^2)^0 = \mathbf{1}$

Any number raised to the power zero equals 1.

Deal or No Deal?

$x^2 - 4y + 55$

Your case

$x^2 + y^3 + 100$

Deal

Your case is valued at "$x^2 - 4y + 55$" dollars and the last remaining case is valued at "$x^2 + y^3 + 100$" dollars. You have an offer to exchange your case for the last remaining case. Both x and y equal -5. What do you choose, deal or no deal?

Dividing Terms with Exponents

When terms with the same base appear in the numerator and denominator, you can simplify the expression by subtracting the exponent of the term in the denominator from the exponent of the term in the number.

For example, $\dfrac{x^5}{x^2} = x^3$, $\dfrac{x^2}{x^5} = \dfrac{1}{x^3}$ and $\dfrac{x^6y^3}{xy^4} = \dfrac{x^5}{y}$

Simplify:

1. $\dfrac{x^8z^9}{x^3z^2}$

2. $\dfrac{8x^3y^7}{-2xy}$

3. $\dfrac{-16x^4y^5z^2}{-24x^4y^3z^3}$

Solution #7

Your case.

If you chose your case, you got the best deal. Here's why:

$x^2 - 4y + 55$ (substitute -5 for x and y)
$= (-5)^2 - 4(-5) + 55$
$= 25 + 20 + 55$
$= 100$ dollars

$x^2 + y^3 + 100$ (substitute -5 for x and y)
$= (-5)^2 + (-5)^3 + 100$
$= 25 + -125 + 100$
$= 0$ dollars

Solution #8

The answers are:

1. $\dfrac{x^8 z^9}{x^3 z^2} = x^5 z^7$

2. $\dfrac{8x^3 y^7}{-2xy} = -4x^2 y^6$

3. $\dfrac{-16x^4 y^5 z^2}{-24x^4 y^3 z^3} = \dfrac{2y^2}{3z}$

16

The Distributive Property

According to the distributive property, $5(x + y) = 5x + 5y$. In other words, multiply the term outside the parentheses by each of the terms inside the parentheses. Give these a try:

1. $4(2x + 3y)$

2. $-3x(4x - y^2)$

3. $-(2x^2 + y - z)$

4. $3xy^2(5y - x^2y^3)$

5. $5(2x - 3y) - 3(y - 3x)$

Don't forget to collect like terms.

7	$4x + 1$	x^2	5	8	3	x	x^0	6
x^3	$1-(-x)$	6	$5x - 3$	$-x + 4$	1	4	$3(x + 1)$	5
$x - 1$	5	2	$2 - (-x)$	9	6	$x^2 + 3$	8	3
3	7	$-1 + x$	2	6	4	$2(3 + x) - 1$	5	$\dfrac{x^7}{x^4}$
5	2	$5 - (-2x)$	$-x + 5$	7	8	1	6	$2x$
6	4	8	$(x + 1)^2$	1	$x^3 - 3$	3	$-2 + 2x$	7
$x^4 - 7$	6	7	8	$3(-1 + x)$	2	5	4	$\dfrac{x}{x}$
4	$4 - (-2x)$	3	1	5	$\dfrac{9x}{x}$	$x + 2x$	7	2
2	1	5	6	$\dfrac{x^5}{x^3}$	$\lvert -9 + x \rvert$	8	3	9

Algebraic Sudoku

We want to fill in the grid so that the numbers 1 through 9 each appear only once in each row, column and 3 x 3 box. Substitute $x = 2$ to find the solution.

The answers are:

1. $4(2x + 3y) =$ **$8x + 12y$**

2. $-3x(4x - y^2) =$ **$-12x^2 + 3xy^2$**

3. $-(2x^2 + y - z) =$ **$-2x^2 - y + z$**

4. $3xy^2(5y - x^2y^3) =$ **$15xy^3 - 3x^3y^5$**

5. $5(2x - 3y) - 3(y - 3x) = 10x - 15y - 3y + 9x$
   $$= \mathbf{19x - 18y}$$

Solution 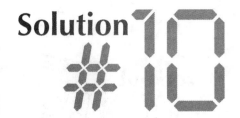 #10

7	9	4	5	8	3	2	1	6
8	3	6	7	2	1	4	9	5
1	5	2	4	9	6	7	8	3
3	7	1	2	6	4	9	5	8
5	2	9	3	7	8	1	6	4
6	4	8	9	1	5	3	2	7
9	6	7	8	3	2	5	4	1
4	8	3	1	5	9	6	7	2
2	1	5	6	4	7	8	3	9

Fact or Fiction?

Workout #11

Directions: Decide whether each of the following mathematical statements or equations is fact (true) or fiction (false). If the equation is false, figure out how to make it true.

1. $(3x^2y)(2xy^4) = 6x^3y^5$

2. $(6x^3)^2 = 36x^5$

3. $(x + 5)^2 = x^2 + 25$

4. $-(2x^2 - 4x + 6) = -2x^2 + 4x + 6$

5. $(3xy^4 + z)$ is a binomial.

6. $\dfrac{x^8}{x^3} = x5$

7. $-1^{19} = -1$

UNIT 2 Equations

Equation Strategy

Workout #12

In order to solve algebraic equations you must cancel terms by performing the opposite operation. Division and multiplication are opposite operations. Addition and subtraction are opposite operations.

Match each equation on the left with the best procedure for solving that equation.

1. $x + 8 = 12$

2. $x - 8 = 12$

3. $8x = 32$

4. $\dfrac{x}{8} = 9$

5. $8x - 8 = 40$

a. divide by 8 on both sides

b. subtract 8 from both sides

c. multiply by 8 on both sides

d. add 8 to both sides then divide by 8 on both sides

e. add 8 to both sides

Solution #11

Here's the truth:

1. $(3x^2y)(2xy^4) = 6x^3y^5$ **Fact**

2. $(6x^3)^2 = 36x^5$ **Fiction**
(When you raise a power to a power, you must multiply exponents. Therefore, the correct answer is $36x^6$.)

3. $(x + 5)^2 = x^2 + 25$ **Fiction**
(When you square a binomial, the result is a perfect square trinomial. If you use the FOIL method, you will see that the correct answer is $x^2 + 10x + 25$.)

4. $-(2x^2 - 4x + 6) = -2x^2 + 4x + 6$ **Fiction**
(Each term at the right should be multiplied by -1. The correct answer is: $-2x^2 + 4x - 6$.)

5. $(3xy^4 + z)$ is a binomial. **Fact**

6. $\dfrac{x^8}{x^3} = x5$ **Fact**

When dividing like terms with exponents, we subtract the exponent of the term in the denominator from the exponent of the term in the numerator.

7. $-1^{19} = -1$ **Fact**
(A negative number raised to an odd power will yield a negative number. An even exponent would give us a positive product. For example, $-1^{20} = 1$.)

Solution #12

The answers are:

1. $x + 8 = 12$ b. subtract 8 from both sides

2. $x - 8 = 12$ e. add 8 to both sides

3. $8x = 32$ a. divide by 8 on both sides

4. $\dfrac{x}{8} = 9$ c. multiply by 8 on both sides

5. $8x - 8 = 40$ d. add 8 to both sides then divide by 8 on both sides

Unit 2 Equations

The Two-Step

When solving two-step equations, start by canceling out the number being added to or subtracted from the variable, then cancel the number that multiplies or divides that variable.

Example:

1. Cancel out the "2" by subtracting it from both sides.

$$3x + 2 = 14$$
$$3x + 2 - 2 = 14 - 2$$
$$3x = 12$$

2. Divide both sides by "3" to cancel out the "3" leaving "x" by itself.

$$\frac{3x}{3} = \frac{12}{3}$$
$$x = 4$$

Directions: Solve the following equations: (Show all steps.)

1. $5x + 8 = 28$

2. $3x - 9 = -3$

3. $\dfrac{x}{4} + 2 = 5$

Unit 2 Equations

Distributor Man

The distributive property tells us that $8(x - 3) = 8x - 24$.

Use the distributive property to remove the parentheses, then solve each equation.

1. $5(x - 3) = 30$

2. $7(y - 4) - 2y = -38$

3. $-2(z - 5) + 3(z - 1) = 9$

Solution #13

The answers are:

1. $5x + 8 = 28$
    $5x + 8 - 8 = 28 - 8$
    $5x = 20$
    $\dfrac{5x}{5} = \dfrac{20}{5}$
    $x = 4$

2. $3x - 9 = -3$
    $3x - 9 + 9 = -3 + 9$
    $3x = 6$
    $\dfrac{3x}{3} = \dfrac{6}{3}$
    $x = 2$

3. $\dfrac{x}{4} + 2 = 5$
    $\dfrac{x}{4} + 2 - 2 = 5 - 2$
    $\dfrac{x}{4} = 3$
    $4 \cdot \dfrac{x}{4} = 3 \cdot 4$
    $x = 12$

Solution #14

The answers are:

1. $5(x - 3) = 30$
    $5x - 15 = 30$
    $5x - 15 + 15 = 30 + 15$
    $5x = 45$
    $\dfrac{5x}{5} = \dfrac{45}{5}$
    $x = 9$

2. $7(y - 4) - 2y = -38$
    $7y - 28 - 2y = -38$
    $5y - 28 = -38$
    $5y - 28 + 28 = -38 + 28$
    $5y = -10$
    $\dfrac{5y}{5} = \dfrac{-10}{5}$
    $y = -2$

3. $-2(z - 5) + 3(z - 1) = 9$
    $-2z + 10 + 3z - 3 = 9$
    $z + 7 = 9$
    $z + 7 - 7 = 9 - 7$
    $z = 2$

22

Variable on Both Sides

Workout #15

When solving equations with the variable on both sides, first simplify the equation by canceling out the variable on one side of the equation.

For example, in the equation "$7x - 8 = 12 - 3x$," we would want to cancel the "$7x$" or "$-3x$." It might be slightly easier to cancel the "$-3x$" by adding "$3x$" to both sides, leaving us with a $10x$ on one side. But it really doesn't matter; the choice is up to you as long as you cancel out one or the other.

Now try these:

1. $8x - 3 = x + 18$

2. $-8y - 20 = 2y + 20$

Once you cancel out one of the variables, you can continue to solve the equation.

$$7x - 8 = 12 - 3x$$
$$7x + 3x - 8 = 12 - 3x + 3x$$
$$10x - 8 = 12$$
$$10x - 8 + 8 = 12 + 8$$
$$10x = 20$$
$$x = 2$$

Classical Music

Workout #16

Classical music refers to music that was composed during a certain period of time. Other music can have a classical style, but it isn't considered classical music unless it was composed during that period. Solve the equations below and put the resulting values of x in the designated places to reveal the period that is considered to be "classical."

$$\underline{\hspace{1cm}} \ \underline{\hspace{1cm}} \ \underset{(c)}{\overset{0}{\underline{\hspace{1cm}}}} \ \underline{\hspace{1cm}} \ - \ \underline{\hspace{1cm}} \ \underline{\hspace{1cm}} \ \underline{\hspace{1cm}} \ \overset{0}{\underline{\hspace{1cm}}}$$

(a) (b) (c) (d) (e) (f)

a. $x - 2 = -1$

b. $-x = -7$

c. $\dfrac{x}{5} = 1$

d. $-2 - x = -3$

e. $-3(2x - 9) = -21$

f. $x + 18 = 24 - 2x$

Solution #15

The answers are:

1.
$$8x - 3 = x + 18$$
$$8x - x - 3 = x - x + 18$$
$$7x - 3 = 18$$
$$7x - 3 + 3 = 18 + 3$$
$$7x = 21$$
$$\frac{7x}{7} = \frac{21}{7}$$
$$\mathbf{x = 3}$$

2.
$$-8y - 20 = 2y + 20$$
$$-8y + 8y - 20 = 2y + 8y + 20$$
$$-20 = 10y + 20$$
$$-20 - 20 = 10y + 20 - 20$$
$$-40 = 10y$$
$$\frac{-40}{10} = \frac{10y}{10}$$
$$\mathbf{-4 = y}$$

Note: Although the side that you chose to cancel may vary, in the end your answers should be the same.

Solution #16

1750 - 1820

$$\frac{1}{(a)} \quad \frac{7}{(b)} \quad \frac{5}{(c)} \quad \frac{0}{} \quad - \quad \frac{1}{(d)} \quad \frac{8}{(e)} \quad \frac{2}{(f)} \quad \frac{0}{}$$

a.
$$x - 2 = -1$$
$$x - 2 + 2 = -1 + 2$$
$$\mathbf{x = 1}$$

b.
$$-x = -7$$
$$(-1)(-x) = (-1)(-7)$$
$$\mathbf{x = 7}$$

c.
$$\frac{x}{5} = 1$$
$$\frac{x}{5} \cdot 5 = 1 \cdot 5$$
$$\mathbf{x = 5}$$

d.
$$-2 - x = -3$$
$$-2 + 2 - x = -3 + 2$$
$$-x = -1$$
$$(-1)(-x) = (-1)(-1)$$
$$\mathbf{x = 1}$$

e.
$$-3(2x - 9) = -21$$
$$-6x + 27 = -21$$
$$-6x + 27 - 27 = -21 - 27$$
$$-6x = -48$$
$$\frac{-6x}{-6} = \frac{-48}{-6}$$
$$\mathbf{x = 8}$$

f.
$$x + 18 = 24 - 2x$$
$$x + 2x + 18 = 24 - 2x + 2x$$
$$3x + 18 = 24$$
$$3x + 18 - 18 = 24 - 18$$
$$3x = 6$$
$$\frac{3x}{3} = \frac{6}{3}$$
$$\mathbf{x = 2}$$

Did You Know?
The best known composers of this period are Joseph Haydn, Wolfgang Amadeus Mozart and Ludwig van Beethoven.

The "Fractionator"

When solving equations with fractional coefficients, multiplying the equation by the least common denominator (LCD) of the fractions will eliminate the fractions.

For example, in the equation $\frac{2}{3}x + \frac{1}{6} = \frac{1}{4}$, the LCD is 12, which is the smallest number that 3, 6 and 4 can all divide into evenly. By multiplying by 12,

$$(12)\frac{2}{3}x + (12)\frac{1}{6} = (12)\frac{1}{4}$$

I'll be back!

we can simplify the equation to $8x + 2 = 3$, which is more manageable.

Directions: Multiply by the LCD then solve.

1. $\frac{3}{4}x - \frac{1}{2} = \frac{11}{2}$

2. $\frac{1}{6}x + 8 = \frac{3}{4}(x - 8)$

Workout #18

Ti<u>x</u> Ta<u>y</u> Toe

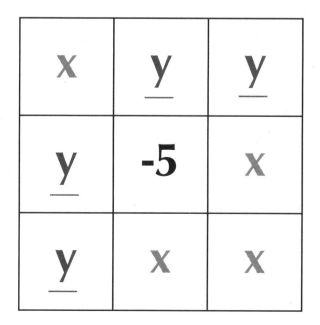

x	<u>y</u>	<u>y</u>
<u>y</u>	-5	x
<u>y</u>	x	x

Directions: Solve both equations to determine x and y. Substitute the values in the grid above to determine whether x or y wins.

$$\frac{-9x}{5} + 3 = -x - 1$$

$$6(y - 3) = -3 + 9y$$

Solution #17

1. x = 8   2. 24 = x

1.

$$\frac{3}{4}x - \frac{1}{2} = \frac{11}{2}$$

$$(4)\frac{3}{4}x - (4)\frac{1}{2} = (4)\frac{11}{2}$$ *(The LCD is 4.)*

$$3x - 2 = 22$$

$$3x - 2 + 2 = 22 + 2$$

$$3x = 24$$

$$\frac{3x}{3} = \frac{24}{3}$$

$$x = 8$$

2.

$$\frac{1}{6}x + 8 = \frac{3}{4}(x - 8)$$

$$(12)\frac{1}{6}x + (12)8 = (12)\frac{3}{4}(x - 8)$$ *(The LCD is 12.)*

$$2x + 96 = 9(x - 8)$$

$$2x + 96 = 9x - 72$$

$$2x - 2x + 96 = 9x - 2x - 72$$

$$96 = 7x - 72$$

$$96 + 72 = 7x - 72 + 72$$

$$168 = 7x$$

$$\frac{168}{7} = \frac{7x}{x}$$

$$24 = x$$

Solution #18

y = -5 wins.

(x)

$$\frac{-9x}{5} + 3 = -x - 1$$

$$-9x + 15 = -5x - 5$$ *(Multiply by 5, the LCD)*

$$-9x + 9x + 15 = -5 - 5x + 9x$$ *(Collect like terms by adding 9x or 5x to both sides.)*

$$15 = -5 + 4x$$

$$15 + 5 = -5 + 5 + 4x$$ *(Add five to both sides.)*

$$20 = 4x$$ *(Divide both sides by 4.)*

$$5 = x$$

(y)

$$6(y - 3) = -3 + 9y$$

$$6y - 18 = -3 + 9y$$

$$6y - 6y - 18 = -3 + 9y - 6y$$ *(Collect like terms by subtracting 6y or 9y from both sides.)*

$$-18 = -3 + 3y$$

$$-18 + 3 = -3 + 3 + 3y$$ *(Add 3 to both sides.)*

$$-15 = 3y$$ *(Divide both sides by 3.)*

$$-5 = y$$

More Fact or Fiction

Workout #19

Directions: Decide whether each of the following mathematical statements or equations is **Fact** (true) or **Fiction** (false). If the equation is false, figure out how to make it true.

1. $\dfrac{4}{0} = 0$

2. If $-x = 3$, then $x = -3$

3. A googol is a number that is equal to 1 followed by 100 zeros and expressed as 10^{100}.

4. In the equation $\dfrac{x}{-4} = -2$, $x = -8$

5. $2x - y - 3x + 5y = -x + 4y$

6. $8(x + 5) = 8x + 13$

7. In the equation $x = -2x + 12$, $x = 4$

8. If $-4x < 8$, then $x < -2$.

Inequalities

Workout #20

When solving inequalities the steps are exactly the same as solving equations, except that when you multiply or divide by a negative number you must reverse the direction of the inequality.

For example, to solve the inequality, $-5x \geq 25$, we must divide both sides of the inequality by -5 and reverse the direction of the inequality. This gives the answer $x \leq -5$.

Solve the following inequalities:

1. $\dfrac{x}{-2} < -3$

2. $6 - 3x > 18$

3. $8 - x \leq -4x + 11$

Solution #19

Here are the verdicts:

1. $\dfrac{4}{0} = 0$ **Fiction**

   (Division by zero is undefined.)

2. If $-x = 3$, then $x = -3$ **Fact**

3. A googol is a number that is equal to 1 followed by 100 zeros and expressed as 10^{100}. **Fact**

4. In the equation, $\dfrac{x}{-4} = -2$, $x = -8$ **Fiction**

   (We must multiply both sides of the equation by -4. Thus, $(-2)(-4) = 8$.)

5. $2x - y - 3x + 5y = -x + 4y$ **Fact**

6. $8(x + 5) = 8x + 13$ **Fiction**

   The distributive property requires us to multiply the 5 by 8 also. Thus, the correct answer is $8x + 40$.

7. In the equation $x = -2x + 12$, $x = 4$. **Fact**

   If you add $2x$ to both sides of the equation then divide by three, you will get $x = 4$.

8. If $-4x < 8$, then $x < -2$. **Fiction**

   When multiplying or dividing by a negative number, you must reverse the direction of the inequality. The correct answer is $x > -2$.

Solution #20

The answers are:

1. $\dfrac{x}{-2} < -3$

   $(-2)\dfrac{x}{-2} > -3(-2)$ *(Reverse Inequality)*

   $x > 6$

2. $6 - 3x > 18$

   $6 - 6 - 3x > 18 - 6$

   $-3x > 12$

   $\dfrac{-3x}{-3} < \dfrac{12}{-3}$ *(Reverse Inequality)*

   $x < -4$

3. $8 - x \le -4x + 11$

   $8 - x + 4x \le -4x + 4x + 11$

   $8 + 3x \le 11$

   $8 - 8 + 3x \le 11 - 8$

   $3x \le 3$

   $x \le 1$

Note: In the last problem, we didn't have to reverse the inequality because we didn't multiply or divide by a negative number. Depending on your steps in solving this problem, you may have had to reverse the inequality. However, your answer should be the same.

How Hot Is It Really?

Celsius and *Fahrenheit* are two different scales for measuring temperature. On the Celsius scale, water freezes at 0°C and boils at 100°C. On the Fahrenheit scale water freezes at 32°F and boils at 212°F.

The formula for converting temperatures from Celsius to Fahrenheit is:

$$C = \frac{5(F - 32)}{9}$$

Use this formula to convert 65° Celsius to Fahrenheit.

Consecutive Order

When solving problems to determine consecutive integers (e.g. 1, 2, 3) use "x" to represent the first; "x + 1," for the second; "x + 2" for the third and so on.

For even or odd integers, use "x," then "x + 2," then "x + 4" and so on.

1. Find three consecutive integers whose sum is 147.

2. Find four consecutive odd integers whose sum is -8.

**149 degrees Fahrenheit.
Wow! That's hot!**

Solution:

$$65 = \frac{5(F - 32)}{9}$$

Multiply by 9, the least common denominator, to cancel out the fraction.

$$9 \cdot 65 = \frac{5(F - 32)}{9} \cdot 9$$

$585 = 5(F - 32)$

$585 = 5F - 160$ (Use the distributive property.)

$585 + 160 = 5F - 160 + 160$ (Add 160 to both sides.)

$745 = 5F$

$$\frac{745}{5} = \frac{5F}{5}$$ (Divide both sides by 5.)

$\mathbf{149 = F}$

Solution #22

1. 48, 49, 50   2. -5, -3, -1, 1

Solutions:

1.
$$x + (x + 1) + (x + 2) = 147$$
$$3x + 3 = 147$$
$$3x + 3 - 3 = 147 - 3$$
$$3x = 144$$
$$\frac{3x}{3} = \frac{144}{3}$$
$$\mathbf{x = 48}$$

Therefore, the next two integers
are 48 + 1 = 49 and 48 + 2 = 50.

2.
$$x + (x + 2) + (x + 4) + (x + 6) = -8$$
$$4x + 12 = -8$$
$$4x + 12 - 12 = -8 - 12$$
$$4x = -20$$
$$\frac{4x}{4} = \frac{-20}{4}$$
$$\mathbf{x = -5}$$

Therefore, -5 + 2 = -3, -5 + 4 = -1 and
-5 + 6 = 1

Slugger

Jorge, the baseball team's top slugger,
has nine hits in his first 23 at-bats.
If he is to have at least a .300 average
at the end of the season,
what is the minimum number of hits
he will need in his final 27 at-bats?

Hint: Batting average is calculated by dividing the number of hits by the total number times at-bat.

Teamwork

If the Blue Squad can clean the beach in 2 hours and the Red Squad can do it in 6 hours, how long would it take both squads working together? Here are some steps to get you started in the right direction:

1. Determine how much of the beach can be cleaned by each squad in one unit of time (an hour in this case). Blue Squad can clean ½ of the beach in one hour and the Red Squad can clean ⅙ of the beach in one hour.
2. Let "x" represent the amount of time it takes both squads working together. Multiply "x" by the amount of beach cleaned in one hour. For example, $x \cdot \frac{1}{2} = \frac{x}{2}$ and $x \cdot \frac{1}{6} = \frac{x}{6}$.
3. With "1" representing the whole beach, set up an equation and solve: $\frac{x}{2} + \frac{x}{6} = 1$

Solution: x = 1½ hours, with both squads working to together.

Now give it a try
without any assistance:

If the Jones crew can paint
a building in 3 days and
the Morris crew can paint
it in 9 days, how long would
it take if both worked together?

6 hits

Jorge's total number of at-bats for the season will be (23 + 27) = 50. He already has nine hits. Let n be the number of hits in his final 27 at-bats. Jorge's final batting average will be the total number of hits, 9 + n, divided by the total number of at-bats, 50. We want that to be at least .300. In equations that is written:

$$\frac{9 + n}{50} \geq .300$$

Multiply both sides by 50.

$$9 + n \geq 15$$

$n \geq 6$ So the minimum number of hits is 6.

2¼ days or 2 days, 6 hours

Let x be the number of days both squads need to paint the building together. Then since the Jones crew can paint ⅓ of the building per day, and the Morris' crew can paint ⅙ of the building per day, we have

$$(\frac{1}{3})x + (\frac{1}{9})x = \frac{x}{3} + \frac{x}{9} = 1$$

$$9(\frac{x}{3} + \frac{x}{9}) = 1 \cdot 9 \quad \textit{Multiply both sides by the LCD.}$$

$$3x + x = 9$$

$$4x = 9$$

x = 9/4 days or 2¼ days

A Snack and a Movie

Directions:

1. Choose any perfect square equal to or less than 100 (1, 4, 9, 16, etc.).

2. Get the square root of the number and then multiply by 9.

3. Now add the digits together. (For example, if you have 23, then add 2 + 3 = 5.)

4. Next, get the square root of your current number.

5. Think of the name of a candy bar or a classic movie that begins with that number.

6. What did you choose?

The Chair Challenge

Today's workout involves a challenge between the boys and the girls. To start, we will need one girl and one boy to volunteer. (Later, others who are interested will get a chance to participate.) The drill is done one student at a time, with the girl going first followed by the boy. Here's what to do:

Standing with their back against a wall, the student will take 2 short foot-length steps away from the wall. Turning to face the wall, the student will bend from their waist, lowering his or her head to rest against the wall. An armchair is placed in front of them next to the wall. The student is to attempt to lift the chair with their arms without moving their heads away from the wall.

Let's get a few other pairs of volunteers to give it try! What's going on here and why? Write your observation and explanation on your workout sheet.

Probable Solution: Three Musketeers

Did you choose the Three Musketeers™?
Chances are you did and so did most of your classmates.
What a coincidence!

Explanation

It did not matter which perfect square you chose that was equal to or less than 100. If you get its square root, multiply by 9 and then add the digits together the result will always be 9. (For example, the square root of 25 is 5. Five times 9 is 45 and the sum of 4 and 5 is 9.) The square root of 9 is 3, leaving you with the word *three* to name a candy bar or a movie. The most popular choice for a candy bar is the Three Musketeers™. For movies, the choice is not quite so obvious. The latest version of *The Three Musketeers* was released in 1993 (well before your time). Perhaps, even some of you selected *The Three Amigos,* which was released even earlier (1986).

I'm sure you've noticed by now that the boys are having a difficult time lifting the chair. In fact, most females can do it, but most males cannot. Isn't that amazing? Why is that?

The reason is simple body mechanics. Most experts believe that it has to do with the difference in the center of gravity. Females have a lower center of gravity than males. Most males find this very difficult because they have already leaned forward past their center of gravity.

Birthday Order

For this workout, we will divide the class into two or three teams, depending upon the size of the class. The teams may be decided by a number of ways including gender, seat location, random pick, etc.

Directions: Silently, without any verbal or written communication, only hand signals, each team is to align its members in the order of their birth months (and date).

After the allotted time (three to six minutes), members of each team will go down the line speaking their birth months and dates. If a member is out of order, the line halts. The team with the most consecutive correct birth months and dates is the winner.

Now, on your workout sheet, make a graph to display a comparison of the number of students on your team who were born in each month.

Let's Tee Up!

Hole	Par	Score	Number of Shots	Cumulative Score in Relation to Par
1	4	Bogey		+1
2	3	Birdie		even or 0
3	5		4	
4	4	Double-Bogey		+1
5	4		5	+2
6	4	Par		
7	3		3	
8	5	Eagle		
9	4		3	
Totals	36			

Golf holes are described as Par 3s, Par 4s and Par 5s. Par is the standard score set for each hole of the golf course. An eagle is 2 strokes less than par. A birdie is 1 stroke less than par. A bogey is one stroke more than par. A double bogey is two strokes more than par.

Directions: For the following nine holes of golf, fill in the blank entries.

All answers will vary.

A bar graph is ideal for displaying this type of comparison data.
A typical graph might look like the following:

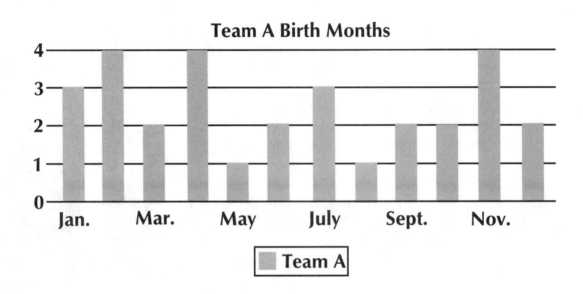

Team A Birth Months

Jan.   Mar.   May   July   Sept.   Nov.

☐ **Team A**

Solution #28

A one-under par 35
is an excellent score.
Now, you're ready
to challenge
Tiger or Michelle.

Hole	Par	Score	Number of Shots	Cumulative Score in Relation to Par
1	4	Bogey	**5**	+1
2	3	Birdie	**2**	even or 0
3	5	**Birdie**	4	**-1**
4	4	Double-Bogey	**6**	+1
5	4	**Bogey**	5	+2
6	4	Par	**4**	**+2**
7	3	**Par**	3	**+2**
8	5	Eagle	**3**	**even or 0**
9	4	**Birdie**	3	**-1**
Totals	36		**35**	**-1**

Eleven . . . Eleven

Workout #29

Do you know how easy it is to multiply by 11? Not just single-digit numbers, but for double- and triple-digit numbers it is simple as well.

Here's how:
To multiply a double-digit number by 11, the first and last numbers remain the same (unless there is a carry) and for the middle number just add the digits together and that becomes your 10s column. For example, 23 x 11 = 253 (2 + 3 = 5) and 36 x 11 = 396 (3 + 6 = 9). When the sum of the two numbers is 10 or greater, just carry the one to the 100s column (49 x 11 = 539).

When you multiply a three-digit number by 11, the product is a four-digit number. The first and last digits remain the same (unless there is a carry) and the 10s column is the sum of the first two numbers (from the right) and 100s column is the sum of the middle and the third number plus any carry. For example, 245 x 11 = 2695 and 139 x 11 = 1529.

Try these without a calculator:
1. 34 x 11 =
2. 72 x 11 =
3. 98 x 11 =
4. 126 x 11 =
5. 248 x 11 =
Bonus: 756 x 11 =

Workout #30

Shopping with Marcy

This weekend at Centertown Mall, Marcy purchased a CD and a poster for $17.50.

If the cost of the CD was four times the cost of the poster, determine the individual prices of the CD and poster that Marcy purchased.

Hint: Think of a method for solving a system of equations.

Solution #29

The answers are:

1. 34 x 11 = 374   (3 + 4 = 7)

2. 72 x 11 = 792   (7 + 2 = 9)

3. 98 x 11 = 1078   (9 + 8 = 17 carry the one)

4. 126 x 11 = 1386   (2 + 6 = 8)
                             (1 + 2 = 3)

5. 248 x 11 = 2728   (4 + 8 = 12 carry the one)
                             (2 + 4 = 6 plus 1 is 7)

Bonus: 756 x 11 = 8316

Solution #30

$14.00

First select variables and write the given information as mathematical expressions. Then solve the equations. For the sake of this example, we'll let "x" represent the cost of the CD and "y" represent the cost of the poster.

$x + y = 17.50$
$x = 4y$
This is a system of equations.

The substitution method will work easily since we know the price of one CD is equal to the cost of four posters (second equation).

Substitute "4y" for "x" in the first equation, then solve.

$4y + y = 17.5$
$5y = 17.50$
$y = \$3.50$ (The cost of the poster)

Therefore, the cost of the CD is:
$x = 4y = 4 \times 3.50 = $**$14.00.**

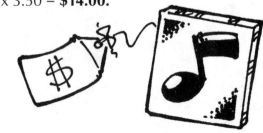

Anyone for Bowling?

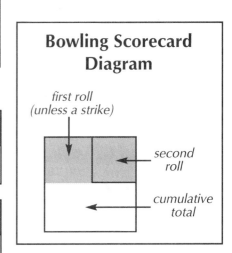

Workout #31

Scoring a game of bowling requires that you learn these symbols:

1. X = a strike (10 plus the number of pins knocked down on the next two rolls);
2. / = a spare (10 plus the number of pins knocked down on the next roll) and
3. - = (miss). For example:

1	2	3	4	5
X	7 2	9 /	5 /	6 -
19	28	43	59	65

Now, score the following game of bowling:

1	2	3	4	5
7 /	8 1	X	5 4	X

6	7	8	9	10
X	6 /	X	- 9	8 / 9

Bowling Scorecard Diagram

first roll (unless a strike)

second roll

cumulative total

Take Five

Workout #32

Directions: Answer the five questions below. Be careful, some may be tricky!

1. How many eights are there in all between 1 and 100?

2. If you read pages 9-31, how many pages have you read?

3. What is 10 divided by $\frac{1}{2}$ then added to four?

4. When four friends get together, each friend shakes hands with each of the other friends. How many handshakes will there be all together?

5. Without looking at the telephone, what are the actual telephone numbers used to dial: 1-800-ALGEBRA.

The score is 167.

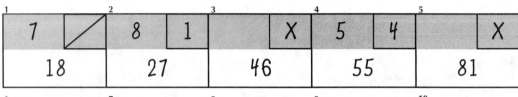

1		2		3		4		5	
7	/	8	1		X	5	4		X
18		27		46		55		81	

6		7		8		9		10		
	X	6	/		X	–	9	8	/	9
101		121		140		149		167		

Good score!
You're almost ready for the pros!

Solution

The answers are:

1. 20
   8, 18, 28, 38, 48, 58, 6**8**, 78, **8**0, **8**1, **8**2, **8**3, **8**4, **8**5, **8**6, **8**7, **8**8, **8**9, 98.

2. 23 pages; don't forget to include page 9.

3. 24; keep in mind that when you divide by a fraction, such as $\frac{1}{2}$, you must multiply by its reciprocal.

4. Six. Keep in mind that a handshake is mutual. When you shake hands with someone that person is also shaking hands with you.

5. 1-800-254-3272. Remember, there are no letters on #1 on the telephone.

The Code

Directions: Match some of the most popular text acronyms with their meanings, then make up a few others for the ones at the bottom.

Workout
#33

___ 1. BFF   a. What's Up?
___ 2. LOL   b. You There?
___ 3. AFK   c. Away From Keyboard
___ 4. HTH   d. Whatever
___ 5. G2G   e. I Don't Know
___ 6. YT?   f. Best Friends Forever
___ 7. IDK   g. Here To Help
___ 8. W/E   h. Be Right Back
___ 9. BRB   i. Got to Go
___ 10. WU   j. Laugh Out Loud

a. Algebra is cool. _____

b. Doing homework. _____

c. Have you solved problem #23? _____

d. When is our next algebra test? _____

e. Can't talk now, because I'm doing algebra homework. _____

Levitators

Today's workout is a mysterious exercise that will astound the entire class. Everyone will get a chance to participate, but first we'll need five volunteers. Let's have one volunteer sit in an armless chair, while the others stand around the chair, two at their shoulders and two at either knees.

Workout
#34

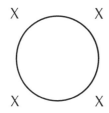

The person sitting in the chair should sit relaxed with both feet together on the floor and their arms folded across their chest. The surrounding four participants should new extend their hands out with their fists clenched together except for their index fingers.

When the teacher counts to three, the four participants will attempt to lift the person in the chair using only their index fingers. Two will try to lift from underneath the armpits and the other two from under the knees. Proceed with caution upon your teacher's count and directions!

Well, what are your thoughts so far? We will try this exercise again shortly, but before we do, we will conduct a power-enhancing hand drill. What effect do you think the drill will have on the next lift? Write your response on your workout sheet.

Solution #33

The answers are:

f.	1.	BFF	f.	Best Friends Forever
j.	2.	LOL	j.	Laugh Out Loud
c.	3.	AFK	c.	Away From Keyboard
g.	4.	HTH	g.	Here To Help
i.	5.	G2G	i.	Got to Go
b.	6.	YT?	b.	You There?
e.	7.	IDK	e.	I Don't Know
d.	8.	W/E	d.	Whatever
h.	9.	BRB	h.	Be Right Back
a.	10.	WU	a.	What's Up?

Here are some suggestions, but you can decide. You're the expert.

a. Algebra is cool. **XCOOL**
b. Doing homework. **HW**
c. Have you solved problem #23? **?23**
d. When is our next algebra test? **XTEST?**
e. Can't talk now, because I'm doing algebra homework. **CTXHW**

Solution #34

Well, let's see what will happen after we do the power-enhancing hand drill. This is how it works:

Moving clockwise, one at a time each of the four lifters will stack their right hand over the head of the person in the chair, keeping their hands two to three inches apart without touching each other's hand or the sitter's head. Then on top of the right hands, the four lifters will stack their left hands on top in the same way. After all eight hands are stacked in line over the sitter's head, the hands are systematically removed one at a time starting at the top. Be careful to remove hands in order and not touch hands. (If a mistake is made, start the drill over.)

Once the hands are removed, the teacher counts to three again and the lifters attempt to lift the person in the chair in the same way as before.

To your amazement, on the second lift the person rises significantly higher and easier than the first time. How amazing!

If you don't believe it, give it a try yourself. Under the direction of the teacher, let's have other volunteers give it a try. Each of you should find the amazing, mystical result.

Now, on your workout sheet, write a few sentences to explain why you think this phenomenon appears to be happening. In other words, is it physically, psychological (all in the mind), mystical (mystery) or something else altogether? Be prepared to discuss your views.

Linear Equations

The solution to a linear equation is a line and all points on the line that make up the solution. A linear equation may have one variable (x or y) or two variables (x and y).

For example, $2x + y = 3$ is a linear equation. Below is the graph of the solution to the equation and the table shows some points on the line. Keep in mind that there are infinite number of points on the line that make up the solution to the equation.

$2x - 3 = y$

x	y
2	1
0	-3
1	-1

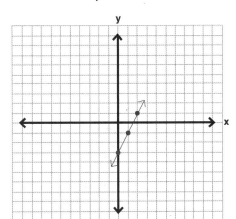

Directions: On your workout sheet, for each problem, complete the table and then use the points to graph the line for each equation.

1. $2x - y = 1$ **2.** $y - 3 = x$ **3.** $y = -x + 2$

x	y		x	y		x	y
1			4				
-1				-1			
0			-2				

Rise over Run

The slope is the steepness of a line. The slope is really a ratio of how many units a line rises (or declines) for each unit it runs (moving left or right).

To find the slope of a line on a graph, just locate any two points on the line and count your way from one point to the next. First by going up (positive) or down (negative), then right (positive) or left (negative).

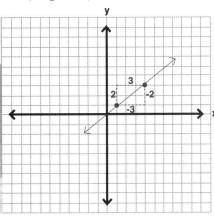

For example, to find the slope of the line to the left, just find the rise over run from two points. If you move from point A to point B, you must go up (+) 2 units then to the right (+) 3 units, giving a slope of ⅔. If you move from point B to point A, you must first go down (-) 2 units then move to the left (-) 3 units, giving a slope of a ⁻²/₃ which is also equal to ⅔.

Directions: Find the slopes of the five lines in the graph below.

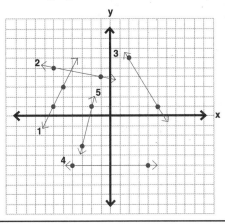

Solution #35

The answers are:

1. 2x - y = 1

x	y
1	1
-1	-3
0	-1

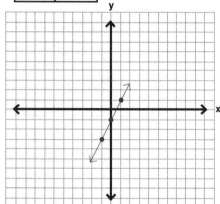

2. y - 3 = x

x	y
4	7
-4	-1
-2	1

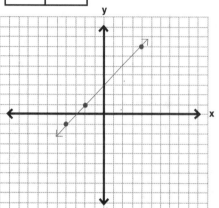

3. y = -x + 2

x	y
1	1
0	2
-1	3

Note: For problem #3, although the choice of points will vary, the graph of the equation should be the same.

Solution #36

The answers are:

1. $\frac{2}{1}$ or 2

2. $\frac{-1}{5}$

3. $\frac{-5}{4}$

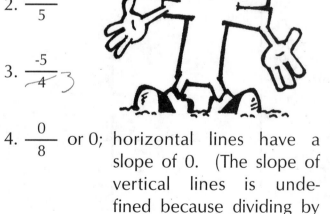

4. $\frac{0}{8}$ or 0; horizontal lines have a slope of 0. (The slope of vertical lines is undefined because dividing by zero is undefined.)

5. $\frac{4}{1}$ or 4

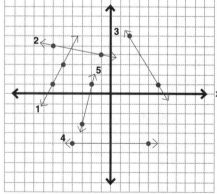

Observe that lines increasing from left to right have positive slopes and lines decreasing from left to right have negative slopes.

44

"m" Is for Slope

The variable "m" is often used to represent the slope of a line. One way of finding the slope of a line is using the following formula:

$$m = \frac{y_2 - y_1}{x_2 - x_1}$$

Given two points on the line, designate one point as your first and the other as your second (it doesn't matter which), then substitute the values into the formula and solve.

Let's use the line with the points (2, -3) and (-4, 5) as an example.

$$m = \frac{5 - (-3)}{-4 - 2} = \frac{8}{-6} = -\frac{4}{3}$$

Directions: Find the slope of the line that passes through the following pairs of points:

1. (4, 5) (2, 3)   2. (-2, -4) (3, 0)   3. $(\frac{1}{3}, -2)$ (-1, 2)

"b" Is for y-intercept

The y-intercept of a line is where it crosses the y-axis. For Line A in the graph shown here the y-intercept is 2. If you compute the slope of Line A, you will find that its slope is ⅓. With the slope and y-intercept you can write an equation for a line.

The variable "b" often represents the y-intercept. The slope-intercept equation for a line is y = mx + b with "m" being the slope and "b" the y-intercept.

Thus, the equation for Line A is $y = \frac{1}{3}x + 2$.

Directions: Find the slope (m) and y-intercept (b) for Lines B, C and D, then write an equation in slope-intercept form (y = mx + b) for each line.

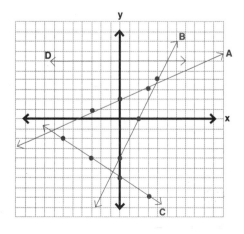

$$1.\ 1;\quad 2.\ \frac{4}{5};\quad 3.\ -3$$

1. $(4, 5)\ (2, 3)$

$$m = \frac{3-5}{2-4} = \frac{-2}{-2} = 1$$

2. $(-2, -4)\ (3, 0)$

$$m = \frac{0-(-4)}{3-(-2)} = \frac{4}{5}$$

3. $\left(\frac{1}{3}, -2\right)\ (-1, 2)$

$$m = \frac{2-(-2)}{-1-\frac{1}{3}} = \frac{4}{-\frac{4}{3}} = \frac{4}{1} \cdot \left(-\frac{3}{4}\right) = -\frac{3}{1} = -3$$

The answers are:

a. $y = \frac{1}{3}x + 2$ (Given)

b. $m = 2, b = -4;\quad y = 2x - 4$

c. $m = \frac{-2}{3}, b = -6;\quad y = \frac{-2}{3x} - 6$

d. $m = 0, b = 6;\quad y = 6$

Note: Horizontal lines have slopes of 0 (zero) and the equations are written with one variable ("y"), while vertical lines have no slopes and the equations are written with one variable ("x"). For example, the graph of the equation "x = 2" is a vertical line crossing 2 on the x-axis.

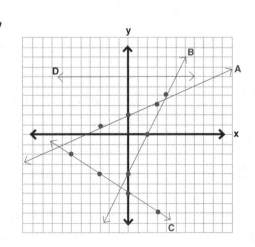

Give Me an "m"! Give Me a "b"!

Given the slope (m) and the y-intercept (b) or any point on a line, you can graph the line. For example, if m = -2 and b = 1, you can graph the line by first plotting the y-intercept on the y-axis, then using the ratio of rise over run, $\frac{-2}{1}$ or $\frac{2}{-1}$, to plot two more points before drawing the line.

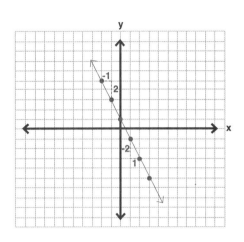

Directions: On your workout sheet, graph the lines given the following information:

1. m = $\frac{1}{4}$, b = -2

2. m = -3, b = 4

3. m = undefined, with the point (-2, -1) on the line.

Using the Slope

By solving an equation for y, the equation will be in slope-intercept form (y = mx + b) with "m" being the slope and "b" the y-intercept. If we solve for "y" in the equation 3x - 4y = 4, we have y = $\frac{3}{4}$ x - 1. The slope m = $\frac{3}{4}$ and the y-intercept b = -1. With the slope and y-intercept we can graph as seen below.

$$3x - 4y = 4$$
$$3x - 3x - 4y = -3x + 4$$
$$-4y = -3x + 4$$
$$y = \frac{3}{4}x - 1$$

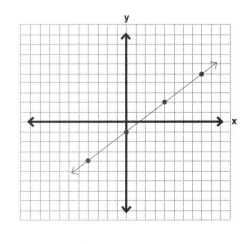

Directions: Write each equation in slope-intercept form, find the slope and y-intercept and then graph the solution to each equation on your workout sheet.

1. 2x + y = -3

2. -3y + x = -6

3. y = 6

Solution #39

Below is the graph of the lines:

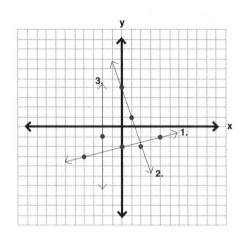

Note: In problem #3 the slope is undefined, therefore the graph is a vertical line. When the slope is zero, the graph is a horizontal line.

Solution #40

The answers are:

1. $2x + y = -3$

$\quad\quad y = -2x - 3$ $\quad\quad\quad\quad m = -2, b = -3$

2. $\quad -3y + x = -6$

$\quad -3y + x - x = -x - 6$

$\quad\quad\quad -3y = -x - 6$

$\quad\quad\quad\quad y = \frac{1}{3}x + 2$ $\quad\quad m = \frac{1}{3}, b = 2$

3. $y = 6$ $\quad\quad\quad\quad\quad\quad m = 0, b = 6$

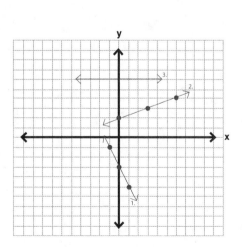

TLC10559 Copyright © Teaching & Learning Company, Carthage, IL 62321-0010

Even More Fact or Fiction

Workout #41

Directions: Determine which mathematical statements are fact (true) or fiction (false). If the statement is false, figure out how to make it true.

1. The slope of the line $y = \dfrac{2}{3}x - 7$ is $\dfrac{2}{3}$.

2. The graph of $y = 3$ is a vertical line.

3. The slope of the line $y = -3$ is undefined.

4. The y-intercept of the line $y = \dfrac{2}{5}x + 1$ is 1.

5. Two parallel lines have the same slopes.

6. Perpendicular lines have negative reciprocal slopes.

7. For the equation $3y - x = 6$, the slope is $-\dfrac{1}{3}$ and the y-intercept is 2.

Graphing Inequalities

Workout #42

Graphing the solutions of inequalities is quite similar to graphing the solutions of linear equations. First, use the slope and y-intercept to graph the line. If the inequality involves < or >, use a full line because the points on the line are considered part of the solution. If the inequalities involves < or >, use a dotted or broken line because the points on the line are not considered in the solution.

The final step is to shade one side of the line or the other. To determine which side to shade, we use a "test point." (Choosing any point on either side of the line as a test point [0,0] is easiest, providing the line doesn't run through the origin). Here is an example of how it all works, using the inequality $2x + y > 3$:

In slope-intercept form, "$-2x + y < -3$" becomes "$y < 2x - 3$" Next, we graph the line with m = 2 and b = -3. Because the inequality involves < or >, we use a broken line. Using (0,0) as a test point in the original inequality, we have $0 > 3$ which is not true. Therefore, we shade the side opposite of (0,0).

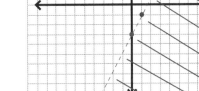

Directions: On your workout sheet, graph the solution to the following:
1. $-3x + y < 2$ 2. $-2x - 5y > 20$

Solution #41

Let's see how well you did:

1. The slope of the line $y = \frac{2}{3}x - 7$ is $\frac{2}{3}$. **Fact.**

   (When you solve for y, the coefficient of x is your slope.)

2. The graph of y = 3 is a vertical line. **Fiction.**
   (The graph of y-equations are horizontal lines and the graph of x-equations are vertical lines.)

3. The line y = -3 has no slope. **Fiction.**
   (The graph of equations with only "y" is horizontal lines with slopes of zero. The graph of equations with only "x" is vertical lines with undefined slopes.)

4. The y-intercept of the line $y = \frac{2}{5}x + 1$ is 1. **Fact.**

5. Two parallel lines have the same slopes. **Fact.**

6. Perpendicular lines have negative reciprocal slopes. **Fact.**

7. For the equation 3y - x = 6, the slope is $-\frac{1}{3}$ and the y-intercept is 2. **Fiction.**

   (Actually, the y-intercept is 2, but the slope is $\frac{1}{3}$. Remember to solve for y.)

Solution #42

The answers are:

1. -3x + y < 2
Slope-intercept form: y < 3x + 2
m = 3, b = 2; broken line;
test point (0,0) 0 < 2, which is true.

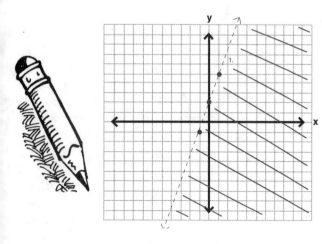

2. -2x - 5y > 20
Slope-intercept form: $y < -\frac{2}{5}x - 4$ (Don't forget to reverse the inequality when dividing or multiplying by a negative number.)
$m = -\frac{2}{5}$, b = -4; full line; test point (0,0) 0 < -4, which is not true.

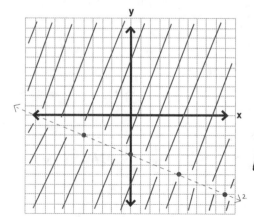

UNIT 4 Linear Equations

The Constitution

A convention of states adopted the Constitution of the United States in its original form in September of what year? Determine the solution to the problems below to find the exact year. *(Remember in y-intercept form, y = mx + b, m = the slope and b = y-intercept.)*

1. Thousands Digit: The slope of the equation $y = x + 5$.

2. Hundreds Digit: The y-intercept of the equation $y - 7 = \dfrac{1}{2} x$.

3. Tens Digit: The slope of the line parallel to the equation $y = \dfrac{2}{3} + 8x$.

4. Ones Digit: The slope of the equation $14x - 2y = 8$.

UNIT 5 System of Equations

Systems

A system of equations consists of two or more equations on a graph. The point of intersection is the solution to the system.

A system of equations may be solved by graphing both equations **(graphing method)**, by using the **substitution method** (substituting the equivalent of one variable in the other equation) or by the **addition/subtraction method** (cancelling out one variable by adding or subtracting the equations together).

For the following systems, determine the best method (graphing, addition/subtraction or substitution) to solve. Explain why you made each of your decisions.

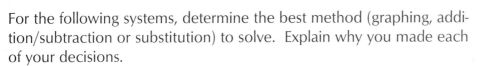

a. $2x - 3y = 6$

   $x + 3y = 12$

b. $y = \dfrac{2}{3}x - 2$

   $y = -\dfrac{1}{2}x + 5$

c. $2x - 3y = 6$

   $x = 3y$

Solution  1787

On September 17, 1787, the Constitution of the United States was adopted by the Constitutional Convention.

1. The slope of the equation $y = x + 5$ is 1, the coefficient of x.

2. The y-intercept of the equation $y - 7 = \frac{1}{2}x$ is 7. If you solve for y, the equation will be written in y-intercept form: $y = \frac{1}{2}x + 7$.

3. The slope of the line parallel to the equation $y = \frac{2}{3} + 8x$ is 8. Parallel lines have the exact same slopes. In y-intercept form, we have $y = 8x + \frac{2}{3}$.

4. The slope of the equation $14x - 2y = 8$ is 7. To get the equation in y-intercept form, we need to subtract 14x from both sides, then divide both sides by -2, which would give us: $y = 7x - 4$.

Solution

a. **Addition/Subtraction Method**
b. **Graphing Method**
c. **Substitution Method**

Here's why:

a. If you were to add the equation together, you can cancel out y, making it easy to solve for x. Once you solve for x, use x to find y (y = 2).

$$2x - 3y = 6$$

$$\underline{x + 3y = 12}$$

$$\frac{3x}{3} = \frac{18}{3}$$

$$x = 6$$
then $y = 2$

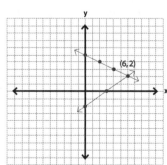

b. Since the equations are already in the y-intercept form (y = mx + b), it might be easier to use the slopes and y-intercepts to graph both equations. The solution or point of intersection is (6,2).

$$y = \frac{2}{3}x - 2 \quad (m = \frac{2}{3}, b = -2)$$

$$y = -\frac{1}{2}x + 5 \quad (m = -\frac{1}{2}, b = 5)$$

c. $2x - 3y = 6$
$x = 3y$

This system is ideal for the substitution because we know x = 3y. Just substitute 3y for x in the first equation then solve.

$$2(3y) - 3y = 6$$
$$6y - 3y = 6$$
$$3y = 6$$
$$y = 2$$

Once you solve for y, use y to solve for x (x = 6).

Solving Systems
(Graphing Method)

Directions: Solve the system of equations using the graphing method.

$$y = -2x + 4$$

$$y = x - 3$$

UNIT 5 System of Equations

Solving Systems
(Addition/Subtraction Method)

Directions: Solve the system of equation using the addition/subtraction method.

$$-2x + 5y = -23$$

$$2x - 3y = 17$$

(3, -2)

$y = -2x + 4$

$y = \frac{1}{3}x - 3$

In the first equation the slope is -2 and the y-intercept is 4. In the second equation, the slope is $\frac{1}{3}$ and the y-intercept is -3. By graphing both equations, the point of intersection is (3, -2). Therefore, this is our solution.

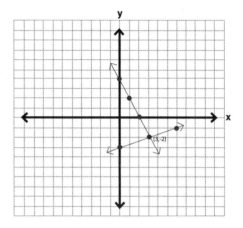

Solution #46

(4, -3)

-2x + 5y = -23 If we add the two equations, the "x" variable cancels out.

$\underline{\quad 2x - 3y = 17 \quad}$

2y = -6

y = -3   By solving for y, we now have part of the solution.

Finally, substitute the value of y (-3) into either equation and solve for x.

-2x + 5(-3) = -23
-2x - 15 = -23
-2x = -8
x = 4

The solution is (4,-3).

Solving Systems
(Substitution Method)

Directions: Use the substitution method to solve the systems of equations.

a. $3x - 5y = -5$

$x = 2y$

b. $x - 2y = 1$

$3y + 5x = 18$

The Sitter

Monique often baby-sits for her cousins, Keyshawn and Opal. Keyshawn's age is equal to three-fourths of Opal's age minus two years. Keyshawn's age plus half of Opal's age is equal to 3. How old are Keyshawn and Opal?

Use the graphing method to solve this system of equation. Use "x" (Opal's age) and "y" (Keyshawn's age) to represent their ages, and write two equations. Find the slopes and y-intercepts of each equation then graph them. The point of intersection gives their ages. How cool is that?

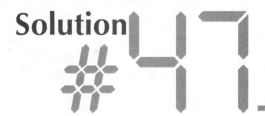
a. (-10, -5)   b. (3, 1)

a.

$$3x - 5y = -5$$
$$x = 2y$$

Because we know that x = 2y, we can substitute "2y" for "x" in the first equation then solve for "x."

$$3(2y) - 5y = -5$$
$$6y - 5y = -5$$
$$y = -5$$

By substituting -5 for "y" in either equation, then solving for x, we determine that x = -10.

$$x = 2y; \quad x = 2(-5); \quad x = -10$$
Solution: (-10, -5)

b.

$$x - 2y = 1$$
$$3y + 5x = 18$$

First, we need to solve for one of the variables in either equation. It's probably easier to solve for x in the first equation, giving us x = 2y + 1.

Substitute (2y + 1) for x in the second equation, then solve.

$$3y + 5(2y + 1) = 18$$
$$3y + 10y + 5 = 18$$
$$13y + 5 = 18$$
$$13y = 13$$
$$y = 1$$

Now, substitute 1 for "y" in either equation, then solve for x.

$$x - 2(1) = 1; \quad x - 2 = 1; \quad x = 3$$
Solution: (3, 1)

Solution #48

Opal is age 4, and Keyshawn is age 1.

Since most of the information is given in terms of Keyshawn's age, it is easier to write the equations in the form of y = mx + b if we let "y" represent Keyshawn.

$$y = \frac{3}{4}x - 2$$

slope m = $\frac{3}{4}$ and y-intercept b = -2

$$y + \frac{1}{2}x = 3 \text{ or } y = -\frac{1}{2}x + 3$$

slope m = $-\frac{1}{2}$ and y-intercept b = 3

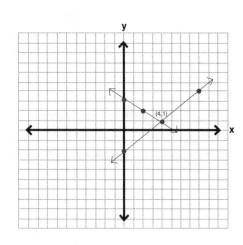

Tricks of the Trade

At first glance, it might not be obvious that the easiest way to solve the system below is to use the addition/subtraction method. However, if you multiply one of the equations by a certain number it will allow you to use the addition/subtraction method to cancel out a variable. Give it a try! *(Remember to multiply on both sides of the equation.)*

$$4x - 3y = 10$$

$$x + 6y = -11$$

Go, Team!

The school's football team won its first game of the season, scoring 52 points. If the team scored twice as many field goals as it did touchdowns (including extra points), how many touchdowns and field goals did the team score?

Solution #49

(1, -2)

There are two options that readily come to mind:

1. If I multiplied the first equation by 2, then I would have 8x - 6y = 20 which would allow me to add the two equations together canceling out y.

2. If I multiplied the second by 4 or -4, I would have 4x + 24y = -44 or -4x - 24y = 44. Either way, I could add or subtract the equations canceling out x.

Either method will work, the choice is up to you.

$$8x - 6y = 20$$
$$\underline{x\ \ + 6y = -11}$$
$$9x = 9$$
$$x = 1$$ Therefore, 1 + 6y = -11 so 6y = -12 which means y = -2.

Or

$$4x -\ 3y = 10$$
$$\underline{-4x - 24y = 44}$$
$$-27y = 54$$
$$y = -2$$ Therefore, 4x - 3(-2) = 10 means 4x = 4 so x = 1.

Solution #50

8 field goals and 4 touchdowns. What a game!

Let's use a system of equations to solve this problem. Use variables to represent what we are trying to determine. (It doesn't matter which variables we use to represent each part of the problem.)

Write two equations for the system, then determine the best method to solve. For the sake of this example, we can let x represent the number of touchdowns scored and y represent the number of field goals scored by the football team. (However, it really doesn't matter which variable we choose to represent each part of the problem. In the end, the answers will be the same.)

As you probably know, a touchdown (with extra point) is worth 7 points and a field goal is worth 3 points. Therefore, the points from touchdowns 7x, plus the points from field goals 3y, should equal the total points scored which is 52. Also, there were twice as many field goals scored as touchdowns or y = 2x.

$$7x + 3y = 52$$
$$y = 2x$$

This problem is ideal for the substitution method. Substitute 2x for y in the first equation then solve.

$$7x + 3(2x) = 52$$
$$7x + 6x = 52$$
$$13x = 52$$
$$x = 4$$

If x = 4, then since y = 2x, we have y = 8.

How cool is that?

TLC10559 Copyright © Teaching & Learning Company, Carthage, IL 62321-0010

Hoops!

Tony, the basketball team's shooting guard,
scored 37 points in the district championship game.
He scored several 3-point and 2-point baskets.
If his number of 2-point baskets were one
more than twice his number of 3-point baskets,
how many 3-point and 2-point baskets did Tony score?

3D

If x plus y equals z;
three times x minus y equals z;
and x is equal to z minus 2,
solve for x, y and z.

Hint: Solve this system in three variables using the addition/subtraction method and/or the substitution method.

eleven 2-point baskets and five 3-point baskets

Let variables represent what we are trying to determine. It does not matter which variable represents the number of 2-point or 3-point baskets.

Let's say that x represents the number of 2-point baskets and y represents the number of 3-point baskets made by Tony.

We can write two equations based on the information given.

$2x + 3y = 37$ (the total number of points scored)

$x = 2y + 1$ (The number of 2-point baskets is one more than twice the number of 3-point baskets.)

This problem is ideal for the substitution method. Substitute "2y + 1" for "x" in the first problem then solve for y.

$$2(2y + 1) + 3y = 37$$
$$4y + 2 + 3y = 37$$
$$7y + 2 = 37$$
$$7y = 35$$
$$y = 5 \text{ (3-point baskets)}$$

If y = 5, then x = 2y + 1 or 11 (2-point baskets)

Solution #52

$x = 2, y = 2$ and $z = 4$

$$
\begin{array}{rl}
x + y = & z \\
3x - y = & z \\
\underline{x = } & \underline{z - 2} \\
5x = & 3z - 2
\end{array}
$$
(Addition method eliminates y.)

We know from the third equation that x = z - 2. Let's now substitute for x and then solve for z.

$$5(z - 2) = 3z - 2$$
$$5z - 10 = 3z - 2$$
$$5z - 3z - 10 = 3z - 3z - 2$$
$$2z - 10 = -2$$
$$2z = 8$$
$$z = 4$$

If z = 4, then x = z - 2 = 4 - 2 = 2.
Since x + y = z, y = z - x = 4 - 2 = 2.

Workout #53

Polynomials

A **polynomial** is one or more groups of algebraic terms separated by plus or minus signs. Certain types of polynomials include:

A *monomial*—one group of terms (e.g. $2x^3y$).

A *binomial*—two groups of terms (e.g. $2xy + 4$).

A *trinomial*—three groups of terms (e.g. $3x^2 + 4x - 7ty^2$).

Directions: Use your knowledge of collecting like terms to add polynomials, horizontally or vertically.

1. $(7x^2 - xy + y^2) + (3x^2 + 3xy - 6y^2)$

2. $(9x^2y + x^2 - 4) + (10x^2y^2 - 11x^2y - y^2)$

Unit 6 Polynomials

Workout #54

Poly-Subtracting-Nomials

When subtracting polynomials, you must change all the signs in the polynomial being subtracted to their opposites then add.

Example:

$(7x^2 - 2x) - (6x^2 + 4x) =$
$(7x^2 - 2x) + (-6x^2 - 4x) = x^2 - 6x$

Now, try these:

1. $(x^2 + 2y) - (3x^2 - y)$

2. $(7a^2 + ab - b^2) - (-7a^2 + 3ab + 3b^2)$

3. $(8x^2y^2 - 11x^2y - 3) - (2x^2y^2 - 11xy^2 + 4x)$

Polynomials may be added horizontally or vertically. However, the key is determining and/or lining up like terms, since these are the only terms that can be added or subtracted.

1. $(7x^2 - xy + y^2) + (3x^2 + 3xy - 6y^2)$

$$\begin{array}{r} 7x^2 - xy + y^2 \\ + 3x^2 + 3xy - 6y^2 \\ \hline 10x^2 + 2xy - 5y^2 \end{array}$$

2. $(9x^2y + x^2 - 4) + (10x^2y^2 - 11x^2y - y^2)$

$$\begin{array}{r} 9x^2y + x^2 - 4 \\ + 10x^2y^2 - 11x^2y - y^2 \\ \hline 10x^2y^2 - 2x^2y + x^2 - y^2 - 4 \end{array}$$

The answers are:

1. $(x^2 + 2y) - (3x^2 - y) =$
   $(x^2 + 2y) + (-3x^2 + y) =$
   $-2x^2 + 3y$

2. $(7a^2 + ab - b^2) - (-7a^2 + 3ab + 3b^2) =$
   $(7a^2 + ab - b^2) + (7a^2 - 3ab - 3b^2) =$
   $14a^2 - 2ab - 4b^2$

3. $(8x^2y^2 - 11x^2y - 3) - (2x^2y^2 - 11xy^2 + 4x)$
   $(8x^2y^2 - 11x^2y - 3) + (-2x^2y^2 + 11xy^2 - 4x)$

$$\begin{array}{l} 8x^2y^2 - 11x^2y - 3 \\ -2x^2y^2 + 11xy^2 - 4x \\ \hline 6x^2y^2 - 11x^2y + 11xy^2 - 4x - 3 \end{array}$$

The FOIL Method

The FOIL method is used to multiply two binomials. FOIL is an acronym meaning "first, outer, inner and last."

Example: $(2x + 3)(x - 5)$

First: $2x \cdot x = 2x^2$
Outer: $2x \cdot -5 = -10x$
Inner: $3 \cdot x = 3x$
Last: $3 \cdot -5 = -15$

Thus, $2x^2 - 10x + 3x - 15 = 2x^2 - 7x - 15$

Now, try these:

1. $(x + 3)(x - 7)$ 2. $(2y - 4)(y - 1)$ 3. $(3x - 2)(3x + 2)$

Difference of Squares

If you were to multiply two binomials in the pattern "$(a + b)(a - b)$" using the FOIL method, the two middle terms would cancel out leaving you with "$a^2 - b^2$," which is a difference of squares.

Example: $(x - 5)(x + 5) = x^2 - 5x + 5x - 25$
$= x^2 - 25$

Now that you recognize the pattern, the process is simple without going through the FOIL method. You simply square the two terms and put a minus sign in between.

Here's another example: $(x + 2)(x - 2) = x^2 - 4$.

Now, try these:
1. $(x + 4)(x - 4)$ 2. $(2x - y)(2x + y)$
3. $(x^2 - 2x)(x^2 + 2x)$ 4. $(3x^2y + xy)(3x^2y - xy)$

Solution #55

The answers are:

1. $(x + 3)(x - 7) =$
   $x^2 - 7x + 3x - 21 =$
   $x^2 - 4x - 21$

2. $(2y - 4)(y - 1) =$
   $2y^2 - 2y - 4y + 4 =$
   $2y^2 - 6y + 4$

3. $(3x - 2)(3x + 2) =$
   $9x^2 + 6x - 6x - 4 =$
   $9x^2 - 4$

Solution #56

The answers are:

1. $(x + 4)(x - 4) = $ **$x^2 - 16$**

2. $(2x - y)(2x + y) = $ **$4x^2 - y^2$**

3. $(x^2 - 2x)(x^2 + 2x) = $ **$x^4 - 4x^2$**

4. $(3x^2y + xy)(3x^2y - xy) = $ **$9x^4y^2 - x^2y^2$**

64

Perfect Square Trinomials

When you square a binomial, the result is a perfect square trinomial. For example, $(x + 3)^2 = (x + 3)(x + 3) = x^2 + 3x + 3x + 9 = x^2 + 6x + 9$.

"$x^2 + 6x + 9$" is considered a perfect square trinomial because the first term (x^2) and the last term (9) are squares and the middle term is (plus or minus) the product of the first and last terms doubled $(3x) \cdot 2 = 6x$.

Now that you recognize the pattern, the process is simple without going through the FOIL method. Take "$(x - 5)^2$" as another example. You simply square the first term to get the first term of your answer (x^2) then square the last term $(-5)^2 = 25$ to get the last term of your answer. To get the middle term, multiply the two terms together ($x \cdot -5 = -5x$) then double it ($2 \cdot -5x = -10x$). Putting it all together, we have $x^2 - 10x + 25$.

Now, try these:
1. $(x - 9)^2$ 2. $(3z + 11)^2$ 3. $(2 - xy)^2$

Multiplying Polynomials

Multiplying by binomials or trinomials is similar to multiplying by a two- or three-digit whole number in that you work vertically from right to left.

Example:

```
      2x² + 3x - 6
 x            x + 3     (1. Start from the right, multiplying "3" times each term of the trinomial.)
      6x² + 9x -18
+ 2x³ + 3x²- 6x         (2. Now, multiply "x" times each term of the trinomial. Be sure to line up like terms!)
  2x³ + 9x² + 3x -18    (3. Add.)
```

Multiply the following polynomials:

```
   3y² - 2y + 5
 x       y - 4
```

Solution #57

The answers are:

1. $(x - 9)^2 = $ **$x^2 - 18x + 81$**

2. $(3z + 11)^2 = $ **$6z^2 + 66z + 121$**

3. $(2 - xy)^2 = $ **$4 - 4xy + x^2y^2$**

Solution #58

The answer is:

$$
\begin{array}{r}
3y^2 - 2y + 5 \\
\times \quad y - 4 \\
\hline
-12y^2 + 8y - 20 \\
+\; 3y^3 - 2y^2 + 5y \quad\;\; \\
\hline
3y^3 - 14y^2 + 13y - 20
\end{array}
$$

UNIT 6 Polynomials

Dividing Polynomials

Dividing by a binomial or trinomial can be done in a way similar to long division. Follow along with this example:

a. "2x" goes into "$2x^2$," "x" times
b. Multiply by "x" times $2x + 1$.
d. Subtract.
d. "2x" goes into "-12," "-6" times
e. Subtract.

$$
\begin{array}{r}
x - 6 \\
2x + 1 \overline{)\, 2x^2 - 11x - 6} \\
-\underline{2x^2 + x} \\
-12x - 6 \\
-\underline{-12x - 6} \\
0
\end{array}
$$

Now, try this one:

$3x + 2 \overline{)\, 6x^2 - 5x - 6}$

UNIT 7 Factual, Exploratory and Logic

Leah's Schedule

Leah has six classes each day: algebra, English, history, science, Spanish and Physical Education. Determine Leah's daily schedule given the following facts:

1. Leah has Spanish just before history and just after English.

2. Her first period teacher wears a lab coat.

3. Leah's favorite class comes last period, just after Physical Education.

4. History is not her favorite class.

2x - 3

Here's how:

a. ("3x" goes into "$6x^2$," "2x" times)

b. Multiply by "2x" times "3x + 2."

c. Subtract.

d. "3x" goes into "-9x," "-3" times

e. Subtract.

$$
\begin{array}{r}
2x - 3 \\
3x + 2 \overline{)\; 6x^2 - 5x - 6} \\
-\;6x^2 + 4x \\
\hline
-9x - 6 \\
-\;-9x - 6 \\
\hline
0
\end{array}
$$

Solution #60

1	2	3	4	5	6
Science	English	Spanish	History	P.E.	Algebra

Hint: One of the best strategies in solving logical reasoning problems involves making a table. By eliminating possibilities using the given facts, the solutions will be obvious.

Statement #1 tells us that Leah has English, Spanish and history in that order. Therefore, English cannot be 5th or 6th period, Spanish cannot be 1st or 6th period and history cannot be 1st or 2nd period.

Statement #2 implies that Leah has science 1st period and that eliminates science from any other period and eliminates other classes from 1st period.

From **Statement #3,** we know P.E. is 5th period, eliminating P.E. from any other period and eliminating the other classes from 5th period.

Statement #4 tells us that history is not 6th period. Now the only possibility for 6th period is algebra. We have three periods unaccounted for. Going back to Statement #1, we know that she has English, Spanish and history in that order, making them 2nd, 3rd and 4th periods, respectfully.

Class	1	2	3	4	5	6
Algebra	x	x	x	x	x	√
English	x	√	x	x	x	x
History	x	x	x	√	x	x
Science	√	x	x	x	x	x
Spanish	x	x	√	x	x	x
P.E.	x	x	x	x	√	x

UNIT 7 Factual, Exploratory and Logic

Computer Terms

Workout #61

Match the terms with the definitions below:

___ cookie   ___ drivers

___ spam   ___ USB

___ SMTP   ___ firewall

a. Mini-programs (instructions) that tell your computer how to use its hardware

b. A way for your computer to connect to external devices

c. A small text file that is placed on your hard drive by a Web server. They are used to keep track of various aspects of your travels through the site in question

d. Unsolicited "junk" e-mail

e. An e-mail protocol that is responsible for moving mail from mail server to another mail server

f. Software or hardware device that protects your internal network from outside threats or unauthorized Internet access from the inside

---

UNIT 7 Factual, Exploratory and Logic

Branches of Mathematics

Workout #62

Can you correctly match each branch of mathematics with its general description?

___ math analysis   ___ statistics

___ calculus   ___ trigonometry

___ geometry

a. Mathematics involving measurements of angles, lines, points, solids and surfaces

b. An in-depth study of functions, combining many of the trigonometric, geometric and algebraic techniques needed to prepare students for the study of calculus

c. Mathematics that studies functions like sine, cosine and tangent

d. Mathematics that deals with differentiation and integration of functions

e. Includes data collection, analysis and interpretation

Solution #61

The answers are:

c. cookie   a. drivers
d. spam   b. USB
e. SMTP   f. firewall

Drivers are mini-programs (instructions) that tell your computer how to use its hardware.

Universal Serial Bus (USB) is a way for your computer to connect to external devices.

Cookies are small text files that are placed on your hard drive by a Web server. They are used to keep track of various aspects of your travels through the site in question. Cookies should be deleted from your computer periodically.

Spam is unsolicited "junk" e-mail. You can consider a message spam if you receive junk e-mail from someone and you never gave them your address.

Simple Mail Transport Protocol (SMTP) is an e-mail protocol that is responsible for moving mail from mail server to another mail server.

Firewall refers to a software or hardware device that protects your internal network from outside threats or unauthorized Internet access from the inside.

Solution #62

The answers are:

b. math analysis
d. calculus
a. geometry
e. statistics
c. trigonometry

Geometry involves measurements of angles, lines, points, solids and surfaces.

Math analysis is an in-depth study of functions, combining many of the trigonometric, geometric and algebraic techniques needed to prepare students for the study of calculus.

Trigonometry studies functions like sine, cosine and tangent.

Calculus deals with differentiation and integration of functions.

Statistics includes data collection, analysis and interpretation.

There is a world of mathematics waiting for you to explore!

TLC10559 Copyright © Teaching & Learning Company, Carthage, IL 62321-0010

Pretty Patterns

Workout #63

Directions: Describe each pattern then find the next two terms.

1. 12, 17, 22, 27

2. 2, 3, 5, 7

3. 1, 4, 9, 16

4. -5, -4, -2, 1, 5, 10

5. -1, $\frac{1}{2}$, -$\frac{1}{4}$, $\frac{1}{8}$

6. O, T, T, F, F, S, S, E

7. 2n + 1, 3n, 4n - 1

UNIT 7 Factual, Exploratory and Logic

Meet Christina's Teachers

Workout #64

Christina's Schedule:

1	2	3	4	5	6
Science	English	Spanish	History	P.E.	Algebra

Each school day, Christina has six teachers: Mr. Chen, Ms. Dumas, Ms. George, Mrs. Martin, Mr. Sanchez and Mr. Williams (not in that particular order). Given the following facts, determine the subject that each teaches:

1. Christina has Mr. Sanchez's class just after her Spanish class and just before Ms. George's class.

2. Just before she teaches her 4th period geometry class, Ms. Dumas has a common planning (class-free) period with Mr. Chen and Mrs. Martin.

3. Mrs. Martin does not teach English.

The answers are:

1. 12, 17, 22, 27, **32, 37** (plus 5)

2. 2, 3, 5, 7, **11, 13** (prime numbers)

3. 1, 4, 9, 16, **25, 36** (squares)

4. -5, -4, -2, 1, 5, 10, **16, 23**
   (plus 1, 2, 3, 4, 5, 6, 7. . .)

5. $-1, \frac{1}{2}, -\frac{1}{4}, \frac{1}{8}, -\frac{1}{16}, \frac{1}{32}$

   (times $-\frac{1}{2}$)

6. O, T, T, F, F, S, S, E, **N, T**
   (**O**ne, **T**wo, **T**hree, **F**our, **F**ive, **S**ix, **S**even, **E**ight, **N**ine, **T**en, . . .)

7. 2n + 1, 3n, 4n - 1, **5n - 2, 6n - 3**
   (Add: n - 1)

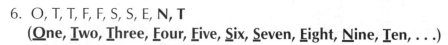

Solution #64

	1	2	3	4	5	6
	Science	English	Spanish	History	P.E.	Algebra
	Mrs. Martin	Mr. Chen	Mr. Williams	Mr. Sanchez	Ms. George	Ms. Dumas

Hint: Remember, one the easiest ways to solve these types of logical reasoning problems is to use a table or grid and eliminate possibilities using the given facts.

From **Statement #1**, we know that Mr. Sanchez teaches history which is just after Spanish and we know that Ms. George teaches P.E. which follows history. This eliminates the other teachers as possibilities for history and P.E., while removing Ms. George and Mr. Sanchez as possibilities for the remaining classes.

Statement #2 reveals that Ms. Dumas teaches math, therefore we infer that she must be the algebra teacher. This eliminates the remaining teachers as Christina's algebra teacher, while removing Ms. Dumas as a possibility for the other classes. Ms. Dumas must have planning 3rd period (before her 4th period geometry). Since Mr. Chen and Mrs. Martin have the same 3rd planning period, we can exclude them as Christina's 3rd period Spanish teachers. Therefore, the only possibility for Spanish is Mr. Williams.

Statement #3: By Mrs. Martin not teaching English, the only other possibility for English is Mr. Chen, therefore leaving Mrs. Martin with science.

Teacher	(1) Science	(2) English	(3) Spanish	(4) History	(5) P.E.	(6) Algebra
Mr. Chen	x	√	x	x	x	x
Ms. Dumas	x	x	x	x	x	√
Ms. George	x	x	x	x	√	x
Mrs. Martin	√	x	x	x	x	x
Mr. Sanchez	x	x	x	√	x	x
Mr. Williams	x	x	√	x	x	x

Trigonometry

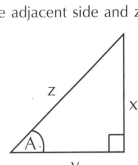

After taking geometry and Algebra 2, you might take a trigonometry course. Trigonometric ratios are ratios of the lengths of the sides of a right triangle:

$$\text{sine (sin)} = \frac{\text{opposite}}{\text{hypotenuse}} \qquad \text{cosine (cos)} = \frac{\text{adjacent}}{\text{hypotenuse}}$$

$$\text{tangent (tan)} = \frac{\text{opposite}}{\text{adjacent}} \qquad \text{cotangent (cot)} = \frac{\text{adjacent}}{\text{opposite}}$$

Directions: For angle "A" in the right triangle below, x is the opposite side, y is the adjacent side and z is the hypotenuse. If x = 3, y = 4 and z = 5, then sin A = $\frac{3}{5}$ = 0.6.

I. Let x = 3, y = 4 and z = 5. Determine the following ratios:
   1. cos A =
   2. tan A =
   3. cot A =

II.
   4. If sin A = .3846 and z = 13, find x (round to the nearest tenth).

Megapixels

A pixel is a single point in an image. A megapixel (MP) is 1 million pixels. For example, a digital camera with 2048 pixels horizontally and 1536 pixels vertically is commonly said to have 3.1 megapixels (2048 x 1536 = 3,145,728 pixels ≈ 3.1 MP).

1536

2048

Directions: For a 4.3 MP digital camera with 1870 pixels vertically, approximately how many pixels does it have horizontally?

The answers are:

1. $\cos A = \dfrac{\text{adjacent}}{\text{hypotenuse}} = \dfrac{4}{5} = 0.8$

2. $\tan A = \dfrac{\text{opposite}}{\text{adjacent}} = \dfrac{3}{4} = 0.75$

3. $\cot A = \dfrac{\text{adjacent}}{\text{opposite}} = \dfrac{4}{3} = 1.333\ldots$

4. $\sin A = \dfrac{\text{opposite}}{\text{hypotenuse}}$

If $\sin A = .3846$ and $z = 13$, then we have the following equation:

$.3846 = \dfrac{x}{13}$

$(.3846) \bullet 13 = x$

$x = 5$ (rounded to the nearest tenth)

Solution  #66

≈ 2,299 pixels horizontally

Solution:

4.3 megapixels equals 4,300,000 pixels which is the product of the number of pixels in the horizontal and vertical directions: total pixels = (horizontal pixels) (vertical pixels).

Therefore, horizontal pixels $= \dfrac{\text{total pixels}}{\text{vertical pixels}} = \dfrac{4{,}300{,}000}{1870} \approx 2{,}299.465$

Logarithms

Logarithms were invented by John Napier about 400 years ago, to make the multiplication and division of large numbers easier. The logarithm of a number is simply the exponent that indicates the power to which a base must be raised to produce that number. For example, $\log_2 8 = 3$ (read "the logarithm base 2 of 8 equals 3") because 2 raised to the 3rd power equals 8.

Example: $\log_3 27 = 3$ (because 3 to the 3rd power equals 27)

Compute the following:

1. $\log_5 25 =$ 4. $\log_3 27 =$

2. $\log_2 16 =$ 5. $\log_2 32 =$

3. $\log_5 125 =$

$\sqrt{\text{Imagine That!}}$

If you try to find the $\sqrt{-25}$ on your calculator, it gives an error message. In the set of real numbers, there is no number that can be multiplied by itself and give you a negative number.

However, this can be done using imaginary numbers (i). The definition states that $= \sqrt{-1} = i$, or $i^2 = -1$. Therefore, $\sqrt{-25} = 5i$, because $(5i)(5i) = 5^2 \cdot i^2 = 25 \cdot (-1) = -25$.

Using the example above, simplify the following:

a. $\sqrt{-36}$

b. $\sqrt{-100}$

c. $\sqrt{-64}$

d. $\sqrt{-144}$

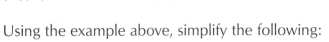

The answers are:

1. $\log_5 25 = $ **2** (**5 to the 2nd power equals 25**)

2. $\log_2 16 = $ **4**

3. $\log_5 125 = $ **3**

4. $\log_3 27 = $ **3**

5. $\log_2 32 = $ **5**

The answers are:

a. $\sqrt{-36} = $ **6i**

b. $\sqrt{-100} = $ **10i**

c. $\sqrt{-64} = $ **8i**

d. $\sqrt{-144} = $ **12i**

More Computer Terms

Workout #69

Match each term with its definition below.

___ POP3   ___ JAVA

___ Google   ___ flash drive

___ PowerPoint   ___ MHZ

a. A presentation program widely used by business people, educators, students and trainers
b. A protocol for getting e-mail off of a Web server
c. The speed of microprocessors, representing one million cycles per second
d. A memory storage device that is typically small, lightweight, removable and rewritable
e. A widely used free search engine that indexes over two billion Web pages in seconds
f. A programming and scripting language that's primarily used by Web designers

---

Mathematicians

Workout #70

Directions: Test your knowledge of famous mathematicians (Banneker, Euclid, Haynes, Hypatia, Newton, Pascal and Pythagoras) by matching them to the following descriptions:

_____ 1. Developed a theorem on the right triangle expressing $a^2 + b^2 = c^2$

_____ 2. First woman to make a substantial contribution in the development of math

_____ 3. Mathematician who founded geometry

_____ 4. Recognized as the first African-American mathematician. Taught himself calculus and trigonometry.

_____ 5. Invented the first calculating device

_____ 6. First African-American woman to earn a Ph.D. in mathematics

_____ 7. Invented calculus and contributed to the understanding of motion, gravity and light

The answers are:

Match the terms with the definitions below:
b. POP3
e. Google
a. PowerPoint
f. JAVA
d. flash drive
c. MHZ

POP3 (Post Office Protocol, Version 3) is a protocol for getting e-mail off of a web server.

Google is a widely used free search engine that indexes over two billion Web pages in seconds.

PowerPoint is a presentation program widely used by business people, educators, students and trainers.

Java is a programming and scripting language that's primarily used by Web designers.

Flash drive is a memory storage device that is typically small, lightweight, removable and rewritable.

MHZ is an abbreviation for *megahertz,* which is the speed of microprocessors, representing one million cycles per second.

The answers are:

Pythagoras (580-500 BC) 1. Developed a theorem on the right triangle expressing $a^2 + b^2 = c^2$.

Hypatia (370-415) 2. An Egyptian woman who was the first woman to make a substantial contribution in the development of math.

Euclid (330-275 BC) 3. Greek mathematician who founded geometry.

Benjamin Banneker (1731-1806) 4. Recognized as the first African-American mathematician. Taught himself calculus and trigonometry.

Pascal (1623-1662) 5. French mathematician who invented the first calculating device.

Haynes (1890-1980) 6. In 1943, Euphemia Lofton Haynes earned her Ph.D. in Mathematics at The Catholic University in Washington, D.C., thus becoming the first African-American woman Ph.D. in mathematics.

Sir Isaac Newton (1642-1727) 7. Invented calculus and contributed to the understanding of motion, gravity and light.

Inventors

Match the inventor/founder with the invention.

___ 1. William Burroughs (1885)

___ 2. Percy L. Spencer (1945)

___ 3. A.S. Douglas (1952)

___ 4. Martin Cooper (1973)

___ 5. Erno Rubik (1974)

___ 6. Raymond Damadian (1977)

___ 7. Robert Jarvik (1978)

___ 8. Larry Page and Sergey Brin (1996)

___ 9. Tony Fadell, Jon Rubinstein and Michael Dhuey (2001)

___10. Dean Kamen (2001)

a. artificial heart

b. calculating machine

c. cell phone

d. computer game

e. Google

f. iPOD

g. microwave oven

h. MRI

i. Rubik's Cube

j. Segway

World Currency

Directions: Match each country with its currency. Be careful, the names of some currencies may be used more than once.

___ 1. Brazil

___ 2. Canada

___ 3. China

___ 4. France

___ 5. Great Britain

___ 6. India

___ 7. Japan

___ 8. Mexico

___ 9. Spain

___10. South Africa

___11. Switzerland

___12. U.S.A.

a. dollar

b. euro

c. franc

d. peso

e. pound

f. rand

g. real

h. rupee

i. yen

j. yuan

Solution #71

The answers are:

b. 1. In 1885, William Burroughs filed the first patent for a calculating machine.

g. 2. In 1945, Percy L. Spencer invented the microwave oven.

d. 3. In 1952, A.S. Douglas wrote his Ph.D. degree at the University of Cambridge on human-computer interaction. Douglas created the first graphical computer game—a version of tic-tac-toe.

c. 4. Dr. Martin Cooper, a former general manager for the systems division at Motorola, is considered the inventor of the first portable handset and the first person to make a call on a portable cell phone in April 1973.

i. 5. In 1974, Erno Rubik invented the Rubik's Cube.

h. 6. In 1977, Raymond Damadian, a medical doctor and research scientist, developed the first full scanner using magnetic resonance imaging (MRI) as a tool for medical diagnosis.

a. 7. In 1978, Robert Jarvik invented the first artificial heart.

e. 8. In 1998 Larry Page and Sergey Brin co-founded the search engine Google.

f. 9. In 2001, the Apple team of Tony Fadell, John Rubenstein and Michael Dhuey completed the iPOD project.

j. 10. In 2001, Dean Kamen created a personal transportation vehicle called the Segway.

Solution #72

The answers are:

g. 1. Brazilian real

a. 2. Canadian dollar

j. 3. Chinese yuan

b. 4. France (euro)

e. 5. British pound

h. 6. Indian rupee

i. 7. Japanese yen

d. 8. Mexico peso

b. 9. Spain (euro)

f. 10. South African rand

c. 11. Swiss franc

a. 12. American dollar

Did You Know?

As of 2007, the euro was adopted in 13 European countries: Austria, Belgium, Finland, France, Germany, Greece, Ireland, Italy, Luxembourg, The Netherlands, Portugal, Slovenia and Spain.

Greatest Common Monomial Factors

The Greatest Common Monomial Factor (GCMF) is the greatest term that divides evenly into a group of terms. For example, the GCMF of $4x^3$, $6x^4$ and $8x^2$ is $2x^2$.

Here's a tip:
In order for a variable to be common to a group of terms, it must be represented in each term. If the variable is present in each group of terms, choose the lowest power of the variable that is present as part of your GCMF.

Here are other examples of the GCMF:
a. For $9x^5y^4$, $12x^4y^3$ and $15x^7y^5$ the GCMF is $3x^4y^3$.

b. For $20x^3y$, $15x^2$ and $10y^2$ the GCMF is 5.
   (x and y are not represented in all terms.)

Determine the GCMF of each group of terms:

1. $4y^3$, $10y^4$, $12y^2$

2. $12x^3y^3$, $16x^4y^2$, $20x^5y$

3. $9x^4$, $18y^3$, $27x^2y^3$

4. $25x^3y^4z^2$, $15x^2y^5$, $3y^3z^4$

Factoring the GCMF

Factoring out the Greatest Common Monomial Factor (GCMF) is like working the Distributive Property in reverse. First, determine the GCMF of the polynomial. Put the GCMF outside a group of the parentheses, then place inside the parentheses the polynomial that could be multiplied by the GCMF to give you the original polynomial.

Here are some examples:
a. $(4x^3 - 8x^2 + 6x) = 2x(2x^2 - 4x + 3)$
b. $(-9x^3y^2 + 12x^2y^3 - 15x^4y) = -3x^2y(3xy - 4y^2 + 5x^2)$
   (If the first term of the polynomial is negative, factor out a negative in your GCMF.)

Directions: For each polynomial below, factor the GCMF.

1. $(20x^4 - 15x^3)$

2. $(12x^3y^3 + 18x^4y^2 - 24y^4)$

3. $(-8x^2z^3 + 16x^3z^5 - 12xz^6)$

Solution #73

The answers are:

1. $4y^3$, $10y^4$, $12y^2$
   GCMF = $2y^2$

2. $12x^3y^3$, $16x^4y^2$, $20x^5y$
   GCMF = $4x^3y$

3. $9x^4$, $18y^3$, $27x^2y^3$
   GCMF = 9

4. $25x^3y^4z^2$, $15x^2y^5$, $3y^3z^4$
   GCMF = y^3

Solution #74

The answers are:

1. $(20x^4 - 15x^3) = \mathbf{5x^3(4x - 3)}$

2. $(12x^3y^3 + 18x^4y^2 - 24y^4) =$
   $\mathbf{6y^2(2x^3y + 3x^4 - 4y^2)}$

3. $(-8x^2z^3 + 16x^3z^5 - 12xz^6) =$
   $\mathbf{-4xz^3(2x - 4x^2z^2 + 3z^3)}$

82

Factoring a Difference of Squares

Factoring a difference of squares is perhaps the simplest factoring pattern if you remember that $(a + b)(a - b) = a^2 - b^2$.

For example, $x^2 - 9$ can be factored as $(x + 3)(x - 3)$.

Directions: Factor the following:

1. $y^2 - 36$

2. $144 - x^2$

3. $25y^2 - 1$

4. $16x^2y^4 - 49z^6$

5. $18x^3y - 2xy^3$ **Hint:** First factor out the GCMF.

Unit 8 Factoring

Factoring Perfect Square Trinomials

In a perfect square trinomial the (plus or minus) first and last terms are squares, and the middle term is twice the product of the square roots of first and last terms. When factored it can be written as the square of a binomial.

For example, $4x^2 + 12x + 9$ is a perfect square trinomial which is equal to $(2x + 3)^2$.

Factor the perfect square trinomials. Be careful, one is not factorable.

1. $x^2 - 16x + 64$

2. $9z^2 + 30z + 25$

3. $25y^2 + 10y + 4$

4. $4x^2 - 4xy + y^2$

5. $72x^3y - 24x^2y + 2xy$ **Hint:** First factor out the GCMF.

Solution #75

The answers are:

1. $y^2 - 36 = (y - 6)(y + 6)$

2. $144 - x^2 = (12 - x)(12 + x)$

3. $25y^2 - 1 = (5y + 1)(5y - 1)$

4. $16x^2y^4 - 49z^6 = (4xy^2 + 7z^3)(4xy^2 - 7z^3)$

5. $18x^3y - 2xy^3 = 2xy(9x^2 - y^2)$
   $= 2xy(3x + y)(3x - y)$

Solution #76

The answers are:

1. $x^2 - 16x + 64 = (x - 8)^2$

2. $9z^2 + 30z + 25 = (3z + 5)^2$

3. $25y^2 + 10y + 4 =$ **Not factorable**
   This is not a perfect square trinomial. The square roots of the first and last terms are 5y and 2, and twice their product is 20y, not 10y.

4. $4x^2 - 4xy + y^2 = (2x - y)^2$

5. $72x^3y - 24x^2y + 2xy =$
   $2xy(36x^2 - 12x + 1) = 2xy(6x - 1)^2$

Factoring Carnival

Simple trinomials could have easily been called the "fun" trinomials because not only are they simple to factor but fun as well—like solving a puzzle.

For example, $x^2 + 5x + 6$ is a simple trinomial. To factor it, find two numbers that you can multiply together to get 6 (the last term) and add together to get 5 (the coefficient of x). Those two numbers are 2 and 3, because 2 times 3 equals 6 and 2 plus 3 equals five. The factored trinomial is: $(x + 2)(x + 3)$.

Note: In the simple trinomial pattern, there is no coefficient for x^2.

Factor the following trinomials:

1. $y^2 + 6y + 8$
2. $x^2 - 5x - 14$
3. $z^2 - 11z + 24$
4. $x^2 + 22x - 75$
5. $3x^2y^3 - 24x^2y^2 - 27x^2y$ **Hint:** First factor out the GCMF.

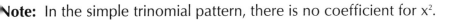

Factor by Grouping

Factorization by grouping is used to factor certain polynomials in four terms. Using the polynomial "$2x^2 + 2x + 3x + 3$" as an example, follow along to see how it is done:

First: Group the terms into two pairs. $(2x^2 + 2x) + (3x + 3)$

Second: Remove the GCMF from each group. $2x(x + 1) + 3(x + 1)$

Third: Notice that the two quantities in parentheses are now identical. We can now factor out the common factor $(x + 1)$ using the distributive property, giving us: $(x + 1)(2x + 3)$

Now try these:

1. $5x^2 + 15x + 2x + 6$
2. $6a^3 - 9a^2 + 2ba - 3b$
3. $2z^2 - 2z + z + 6$

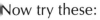

Solution #77

The answers are:

1. $y^2 + 6y + 8 = \textbf{(y + 4)(y + 2)}$

2. $x^2 - 5x - 14 = \textbf{(x - 7)(x + 2)}$

3. $z^2 - 11z + 24 = \textbf{(z - 8)(z - 3)}$

4. $x^2 + 22x - 75 = \textbf{(x + 25)(x - 3)}$

5. $3x^2y^3 - 24x^2y^2 - 27x^2y = \textbf{3x}^2\textbf{y(y}^2\textbf{ - 8y - 9)} = \textbf{3x}^2\textbf{y(y - 9)(y + 1)}$

Solution #78

The answers are:

1. $5x^2 + 15x + 2x + 6$
   $(5x^2 + 15x) + (2x + 6)$
   $5x(x + 3) + 2(x + 3)$
   $\textbf{(5x + 2)(x + 3)}$

2. $6a^3 - 9a^2 + 2ba - 3b$
   $(6a^3 - 9a^2) + (2ba - 3b)$
   $3a^2(2a - 3) + b(2a - 3)$
   $\textbf{(3a}^2\textbf{ + b)(2a - 3)}$

3. $2z^2 - 2z + z - 1$
   $(2z^2 - 2z) + (z - 1)$
   $2z(z - 1) + 1(z - 1)$
   $\textbf{(2z + 1)(z - 1)}$

General Trinomials

General trinomials are in the form $ax^2 + bx + c$. For example, $6x^2 + 11x + 4$ is a general trinomial. Perhaps, the simplest method of factoring general trinomials is the factor by grouping method. Here is how it's done:

First: Find the grouping number by multiplying a • c. In the case of "$6x^2 + 11x + 4$," the grouping number is 6 • 4 = 24.

Second: Find two numbers that we can multiply together to get 24 and add together to get b, which is 11 in this problem. Those numbers are 3 and 8 because 3 • 8 = 24 and 3 + 8 = 11.

Third: Rewrite the trinomial into four terms, substituting 3x + 8x for 11x, thus now having "$6x^2 + 3x + 8x + 4$."

Fourth: Proceed to factor by group:
$(6x^2 + 3x) + (8x + 4) = 3x(2x + 1) + 4(2x + 1)$

Answer: $= (2x + 1)(3x + 4)$

Factor the following general trinomials:

1. $2x^2 + 9x + 10$

2. $3x^2 + 10x - 8$

A Factoring Medley

Factoring completely involves considering all possible factoring patterns, starting with the Greatest Common Monomial Factor (GCMF). After the GCMF, it is recommended that you look for the following patterns in this order:

a. Difference of Squares, for example: $x^2 - 4 = (x + 2)(x - 2)$

b. Perfect Square Trinomials, for example: $4x^2 - 12x + 9 = (2x - 3)^2$

c. Simple Trinomials, for example: $x^2 - 7x - 18 = (x - 9)(x + 2)$

d. General Trinomials, for example: $4x^2 - 11x - 3 = (4x + 1)(x - 3)$

Completely factor the following polynomials:

1. $3xy^3 - 12xy^2 + 9xy$ 2. $6x^2y + 8xy - 8y$ 3. $x^5y - xy$

Solution #79

The answers are:

1. $2x^2 + 9x + 10$

First: Grouping Number = 2 • 10 = 20

Second: Two numbers are 4 and 5 (since 4 • 5 = 20 and 4 + 5 = 9)

Third: $2x^2 + 4x + 5x + 10$

Fourth: $(2x^2 + 4x) + (5x + 10)$
= $(2x(x + 2) + 5(x + 2)$
= **$(2x + 5)(x + 2)$**

2. $3x^2 + 10x - 8$

First: Grouping Number = 3 • -8 = -24.

Second: Two numbers are 12 and -2 (since 12 • -2 = -24 and 12 + -2 = 10)

Third: $3x^2 + 12x - 2x - 8$

Fourth: $(3x^2 + 12x) - (2x + 8)$
= $3x(x + 4) - 2(x + 4)$
= **$(3x - 2)(x + 4)$**

Solution #80

The answers are:

1.

	$3xy^3 - 12xy^2 + 9xy =$
GCMF	$3xy(y^2 - 4y + 3) =$
Simple Trinomial	**$3xy(y - 3)(y - 1)$**

3.

	$x^5y - xy$
GCMF	$xy(x^4 - 1)$
Difference of Squares	$xy(x^2 - 1)(x^2 + 1)$
Another Difference of Squares	**$xy(x + 1)(x - 1)(x^2 + 1)$**

2.

	$6x^2y + 8xy - 8y$
GCMF	$2y(3x^2 + 4x - 4)$
General Trinomial:	$2y[(3x^2 + 6x) - (2x + 4)]$
Grouping Number	$2y[(3x)(x + 2) - 2(x + 2)]$
is 3 • -4 = -12;	**$2y(3x - 2)(x + 2)$**
use 6, -2	

88

Triangles and Rectangles

Today's workout will require us to use our algebraic skills in solving problems pertaining to the triangle and rectangle.

1. The formula for the area of a triangle is:
   $a = \frac{1}{2} bh$.   Solve this formula in terms of h.
   (In other words, get "h" alone on one side of the equation.)

2. If the perimeter of the rectangle below is 38 cm, find its length and width.

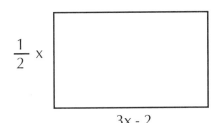

$\frac{1}{2}$ x

3x - 2

Lines, Rays and Planes

Match the following terms with the definitions below:

a. angle   b. line   c. plane   d. point
e. postulate   f. ray   g. segment   h. theorem

_____ 1. A statement assumed to be true without proof

_____ 2. A flat surface that stretches into infinity

_____ 3. A straight set of points that extends into infinity in both directions

_____ 4. Part of a line that has one endpoint and extends to infinity in one direction

_____ 5. An important mathematical statement which can be proven using postulates, definitions and previously proved theorems

_____ 6. A location in geometry that has no dimensions

_____ 7. The union of two rays that have the same endpoint

_____ 8. Two points on a line and all the points between those two points

Solution #81

The answers are:

1. $a = \frac{1}{2} bh$.

    $2a = bh$ *(To cancel out the fraction, multiply by 2, the least common denominator.)*

    $\frac{2a}{b} = \frac{bh}{b}$

    $\frac{2a}{b} = h$

2. The perimeter is the sum of the two lengths and two widths, which we are told is 38 cm. We can write that as an equation:

$$\frac{1}{2}x + \frac{1}{2}x + (3x - 2) + (3x - 2) = 38$$

$7x - 4 = 38$ (Collect like terms.)
$7x - 4 + 4 = 38 + 4$ (Add 4 to both sides.)
$7x = 42$
$\frac{7x}{7} = \frac{42}{7}$
$x = 6$

Next, use $x = 6$ to determine the width and the length.
width $= \frac{1}{2}x = \frac{1}{2}(6) = $ **3 cm**
length $= 3x - 2 = 3(6) - 2 = $ **16 cm**

Solution #82

The answers are:

1. **e.** A **postulate** is a statement assumed to be true without proof.

2. **c.** A **plane** is a flat surface that stretches into infinity.

3. **b.** A **line** is a straight set of points that extends into infinity in both directions.

4. **f.** A **ray** is a part of a line that has one endpoint and extends to infinity in one direction.

5. **h.** A **theorem** is an important mathematical statement which can be proven using postulates, definitions and previously proved theorems.

6. **d.** A **point** is a location in geometry that has no dimensions.

7. **a.** An **angle** is the union of two rays that have the same endpoint.

8. **g.** A **segment** consists of two points on a line, and all the points between those two points.

90

Workout #83

Circles

Please solve the following two problems involving the circle:

1. The **circumference** of a circle is: $C = \pi d$. Find the diameter of a circle with a circumference of 25.12 cm. (For π use 3.14.)

2. The **area** of a circle is: $A = \pi r^2$. Find the diameter of a circle with an area of 78.5 cm^2.

Unit 9 Pre-Geometry

Workout #84

Degrees of Kevin Polygon

A **polygon** is a closed shape consisting of line segments. Triangles and quadrilaterals are examples of polygons.

The number of degrees in the sum of the interior angles of a polygon is determined by subtracting two from its number of sides, S, and then multiplying by 180: Degrees = 180(S - 2).

For example, a triangle has three sides and, therefore the sum of its three interior angles is: Degrees = 180 (3 – 2) = 180(1) = 180 degrees.

Determine the number of degrees in the following polygons:

1. pentagon
2. octagon
3. hectogon **Hint:** *Hecto* comes from a Greek word that means "a hundred."

Solution #83

The answers are:

1. **8 cm**

$$C = \pi d$$
$$25.12 = 3.14d$$
$$\frac{25.12}{3.14} = \frac{3.14d}{3.14}$$
$$8 = d$$

2. **10 cm**

$$A = \pi r^2$$
$$78.5 = 3.14r^2$$
$$\frac{78.5}{3.14} = \frac{3.14r^2}{3.14}$$
$$25 = r^2$$
$$\sqrt{25} = \sqrt{r^2}$$
$$5 = r$$

If the radius is 5 cm, then the diameter equals 10 cm (d = 2r).

Solution #84

The answers are:

1. For a pentagon, a five-sided polygon, we have
   180 x (5 - 2) = 180 x 3 = **540 degrees**.

2. For an octagon, an eight-sided polygon, we have
   180 x (8 - 2) = 180 x 6 = **1,080 degrees**.

3. For a hectagon, a 100-sided polygon, we have
   180 x (100 - 2) = 180 x 98 = **17,640 degrees**.

Unit 9 Pre-Geometry

More Math Signs and Symbols

Workout #85

Match the sign or symbol with its meaning:

a. $\cong$ b. ∞ c. !   d. $\perp$

e. $\sqrt{}$ f. $\angle$ g. $||$ h. $f(x)$

____ 1. parallel

____ 2. congruent

____ 3. function

____ 4. angle

____ 5. factorial

____ 6. a 90 degree or right angle

____ 7. infinity

____ 8. perpendicular

Unit 10 Radicals

$\sqrt{}$ Radically Speaking!

Workout #86

The **square root** of a number is another number which, when multiplied by itself, produces the original number.   The symbol for a square root is the radical ($\sqrt{}$).

Examples:

a. $\sqrt{49} = 7$ b. $\sqrt{x^6} = x^3$ c. $\sqrt{25x^4} = 5x^2$

Find the square roots of the following numbers:

1. $\sqrt{100}$ 2. $\sqrt{x^2y^4}$

3. $\sqrt{64x^6y^{10}}$ 4. $\sqrt{169x^{14}y^2z^8}$

5. $\sqrt{\dfrac{1}{4}}$ 6. $\sqrt{0.36x^4}$

Solution #85

The answers are:

g. $||$ 1. parallel

a. $\cong$ 2. congruent (exactly the same)

h. $f(x)$ 3. function (the value of the function f at the element x)

f. $\angle$ 4. angle

c. $!$ 5. factorial (for example, $3! = 3 \cdot 2 \cdot 1 = 6$)

e. $\lrcorner$ 6. a 90 degree or right angle

b. ∞ 7. infinity

d. $\perp$ 8. perpendicular (forming a 90 degree angle)

Solution #86

The answers are:

1. $\sqrt{100} = \mathbf{10}$

2. $\sqrt{x^2 y^4} = \mathbf{xy^2}$

3. $\sqrt{64x^6 y^{10}} = \mathbf{8x^3 y^5}$

4. $\sqrt{169x^{14} y^2 z^8} = \mathbf{13x^7 yz^4}$

5. $\sqrt{\dfrac{1}{4}} = \mathbf{\dfrac{1}{2}}$

6. $\sqrt{0.36x^4} = \mathbf{0.6x^2}$

94

Workout #87

Dude, this is Radical!

When the radicand is not a prefect square, break it down into the product of two radicals: one for the GCF (Greatest Common Factor) that is a perfect square and the other for the remaining factor. Then simplify.

DUDE

Examples:

a. $\sqrt{x^5} = \sqrt{x^4}\ \sqrt{x} = x^2\ \sqrt{x}$

b. $\sqrt{8x^3} = \sqrt{4x^2}\ \sqrt{2x} = 2x\ \sqrt{2x}$

Give these a try:

1. $\sqrt{x^7} =$ 2. $\sqrt{4x^5} =$

3. $\sqrt{x^7y^9} =$ 4. $\sqrt{27y^4x^3} =$

5. $\sqrt{98x^9y^{11}z} =$

Simply Radical

3xy

Workout #88

Adding and subtracting expressions containing radicals is collecting two like terms, provided the terms beneath the radical (known as the radicand) are the same.

Examples:

a. $2\ \sqrt{3} + 5\ \sqrt{3} = 7\ \sqrt{3}$

b. $4\ \sqrt{x} + \sqrt{y} - \sqrt{x} = 3\ \sqrt{x} + \sqrt{y}$

Simplify:

1. $3\ \sqrt{2} + 2\ \sqrt{2} + \sqrt{2} =$ 2. $6\ \sqrt{x} - \sqrt{x} =$

3. $\sqrt{3} - 4\ \sqrt{3} + 2\ \sqrt{3} =$ 4. $\sqrt{11} + \sqrt{7} + \sqrt{11} - 3\ \sqrt{7} =$

Solution #87

The answers are:

1. $\sqrt{x^7} = \sqrt{x^6}\,\sqrt{x} = x^3\,\sqrt{x}$

2. $\sqrt{4x^5} = \sqrt{4x^4}\,\sqrt{x} = 2x^2\,\sqrt{x}$

3. $\sqrt{x^7y^9} = \sqrt{x^6y^8}\,\sqrt{xy} = x^3y^4\,\sqrt{xy}$

4. $\sqrt{27y^4x^3} = \sqrt{9y^4x^2}\,\sqrt{3x} = 3y^2x\,\sqrt{3x}$

5. $\sqrt{98x^9y^{11}z} = \sqrt{49x^8y^{10}}\,\sqrt{2xyz} = 7x^4y^5\,\sqrt{2xyz}$

Solution #88

The answers are:

1. $3\,\sqrt{2} + 2\,\sqrt{2} + \sqrt{2} = 6\,\sqrt{2}$

2. $6\,\sqrt{x} - \sqrt{x} = 5\,\sqrt{x}$

3. $\sqrt{3} - 4\,\sqrt{3} + 2\,\sqrt{3} = -\,\sqrt{3}$

4. $\sqrt{11} + \sqrt{7} + \sqrt{11} - 3\,\sqrt{7} = 2\,\sqrt{11} - 2\,\sqrt{7} = 2(\sqrt{11} - \sqrt{7})$

96

UNIT 10 Radicals

$$\sqrt{a} \cdot \sqrt{b} = \sqrt{ab}$$
Radical Rule

The rule above makes multiplying radicals easy.
Here are some examples:

a. $\sqrt{3} \cdot \sqrt{2} = \sqrt{6}$

b. $3\sqrt{2} \cdot 2\sqrt{8} = (3 \cdot 2)\sqrt{2 \cdot 8} = 6\sqrt{16}$

Multiply and simplify the following expres

1. $\sqrt{7} \cdot \sqrt{3} =$

2. $3\sqrt{5} \cdot 4\sqrt{7} =$

3. $\sqrt{3} \cdot \sqrt{12} =$

4. $2\sqrt{2} \cdot 5\sqrt{6} =$

5. $(\sqrt{3} + 2)(\sqrt{3} - 2) =$

UNIT 10 Radicals

$\sqrt{\text{Fact}}$ or $\sqrt{\text{Fiction}}$?

1. $x^0 = 1$

2. $2^{-3} = -8$

3. $111,111,111 \times 111,111,111 = 12,345,678,987,654,321$

4. $\sqrt{y^6} = y^3$

5. $\sqrt{x^5} = x^2\sqrt{x}$

6. $\sqrt{x} + \sqrt{y} = \sqrt{xy}$

7. $2\sqrt{3} + \sqrt{3} = 3\sqrt{3}$

8. $\sqrt{12} \cdot \sqrt{3} = 6$

Solution #89

The answers are:

1. $\sqrt{7} \cdot \sqrt{3} = \sqrt{21}$

2. $3\sqrt{5} \cdot 4\sqrt{7} = (3 \cdot 4)\sqrt{5 \cdot 7} = 12\sqrt{35}$

3. $\sqrt{3} \cdot \sqrt{12} = \sqrt{3 \cdot 12} = \sqrt{36} = 6$

4. $2\sqrt{2} \cdot 5\sqrt{6} = (2 \cdot 5)\sqrt{2 \cdot 6} = 10\sqrt{12}$
   $$= 10\sqrt{4}\sqrt{3}$$
   $$= 20\sqrt{3}$$

5. $(\sqrt{3} + 2)(\sqrt{3} - 2) =$
   Using the FOIL method, we have:
   $\sqrt{3}\sqrt{3} - 2\sqrt{3} + 2\sqrt{3} - 4 = 3 - 4 = -1$

Solution #90

The answers are:

1. $x^0 = 1$ **Fact** (By definition, any real number raised to the zero power equals 1.)

2. $2^{-3} = -8$ **Fiction** By definition, $x^{-y} = \dfrac{1}{x^y}$. So $2^{-3} = \dfrac{1}{2^3} = \dfrac{1}{8}$.

3. $111,111,111 \times 111,111,111 = 12,345,678,987,654,321$ **Fact**

4. $\sqrt{y^6} = y^3$ **Fact**

5. $\sqrt{x^5} = x^2\sqrt{x}$ **Fact** $\sqrt{x^5} = \sqrt{x^4}\sqrt{x} = x^2\sqrt{x}$

6. $\sqrt{x} + \sqrt{y} = \sqrt{xy}$ **Fiction** (These are considered unlike terms, therefore cannot be simplified further.

7. $2\sqrt{3} + \sqrt{3} = 3\sqrt{3}$ **Fact**

8. $\sqrt{12} \cdot \sqrt{3} = 6$ **Fact** $\sqrt{12} \cdot \sqrt{3} = \sqrt{12 \cdot 3} = \sqrt{36} = 6$

98

TLC10559 Copyright © Teaching & Learning Company, Carthage, IL 62321-0010

Rationalizing the Denominator

People often do not like to have fractions with radicals in the denominator, like $\frac{2}{\sqrt{3}}$.

In order to "rationalize" the denominator, we need to get rid of all radicals that are in the denominator. The easier way to do this is to multiply both numerator and denominator by the square root of an expression that will give us a perfect square under the radical in the denominator. For example:

$$\frac{2}{\sqrt{3}} = \frac{2}{\sqrt{3}} \cdot \frac{\sqrt{3}}{\sqrt{3}} = \frac{2\sqrt{3}}{3}$$

Try rationalizing the denominator in the following expressions:

1. $\dfrac{3}{\sqrt{5}}$

2. $\dfrac{3\sqrt{8}}{\sqrt{2}}$

3. $\dfrac{2\sqrt{3}}{\sqrt{3}+1}$ **Hint:** Think "difference of squares."

The Root of the Problem

You know that $\sqrt{25}$ stands for the number that multiplied by itself equals 25 (i.e. $\sqrt{25} = 5$ because $5 \cdot 5 = 25$).

$\sqrt[3]{8}$ stands for the number that gives 8 when multiplied by itself 3 times. Thus, $\sqrt[3]{8} = 2$ because $2 \cdot 2 \cdot 2 = 8$.

Find the following roots:

1. $\sqrt[3]{125}$ 2. $\sqrt[3]{1000}$

3. $\sqrt[3]{64x^6}$ 4. $\sqrt[4]{16}$

The answers are:

1. $\dfrac{3}{\sqrt{5}} \cdot \dfrac{\sqrt{5}}{\sqrt{5}} = \dfrac{3\sqrt{5}}{5}$

2. $\dfrac{3\sqrt{8}}{\sqrt{2}} \cdot \dfrac{\sqrt{2}}{\sqrt{2}} = \dfrac{3\sqrt{16}}{\sqrt{4}} = \dfrac{3 \cdot 4}{2} = \dfrac{12}{2} = 6$

3. $\dfrac{2\sqrt{3}}{\sqrt{3}+1} \cdot \dfrac{\sqrt{3}-1}{\sqrt{3}-1} = \dfrac{2\sqrt{3}(\sqrt{3}-1)}{(\sqrt{3}+1)(\sqrt{3}-1)} = \dfrac{2\sqrt{3}\sqrt{3}-2\sqrt{3}}{\sqrt{3}\sqrt{3}-\sqrt{3}+\sqrt{3}-1)}$

(In the numerator, we multiplied using the distributive property, and in the denominator we used the FOIL method to multiply.)

$= \dfrac{6-2\sqrt{3}}{3-1} = 3 - \sqrt{3}$ **Notice:** The middle terms cancel out like in a difference of squares.

The answers are:

1. $\sqrt[3]{125} = 5$
   $(5 \cdot 5 \cdot 5 = 125)$

2. $\sqrt[3]{1000} = 10$
   $(10 \cdot 10 \cdot 10 = 100)$

3. $\sqrt[3]{64x^6} = 4x^2$
   $(4x^2 \cdot 4x^2 \cdot 4x^2 = 64x^6)$

4. $\sqrt[4]{16} = 2$
   $(2 \cdot 2 \cdot 2 \cdot 2 = 16)$

PSAT Prep Introduction

PSAT stands for "Preliminary SAT." The SAT is a standardized test for college admissions in the United States. The PSAT tests critical reading, math problem solving and writing skills. The test is offered in October. Most students take the PSAT their junior year of high school. However, it is also recommended that you take the test as a sophomore as well. The PSAT is good practice for the SAT, which contains the same type of questions.

Directions: Solve the following PSAT prep problems:

1. For what values of a and b is $(a \times b) < 0$?
   a. $a = 4, b = 0.0001$
   b. $a = 3, b = 0.0001$
   c. $a = 0, b = -7$
   d. $a = -2, b = 4$
   e. $a = -3, b = -12$

2. For which ordered pair is $2x^2 - y = 10$
   a. $(2, 2)$
   b. $(-2, 2)$
   c. $(0, 10)$
   d. $(-2, -2)$
   e. $(1, 8)$

Grid-In

The PSAT math portion consists of two 25-minute sections: 28 multiple-choice questions and 10 grid-ins. The grid-ins are not multiple-choice and must be filled in. There will be no negative numbers or mixed numbers as answers. (Mixed numbers must be converted to improper fractions or decimals.) Unlike the multiple-choice section, the grid-in section does not penalize for wrong answers.

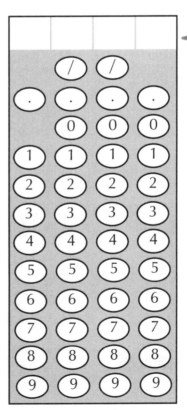

Directions: Solve the following problem, then grid-in your answer on your workout sheet.

1. If $4^{n+2} = 64$, what does n equal?
2. If $8x = 2x + 3$, then $3x + 5 =$

1. D; 2. D

1. If the product of two numbers is negative, then one would have to be positive and one would have to be negative. Therefore the correct answer is d. (a = -2, b = 4).

2. Substitute the values of each ordered pair into the equation to determine which is the solution.

a. $2(2)^2 - 2 = 6$ No
b. $2(-2)^2 - 2 = 6$ No
c. $2(0)^2 - 10 = -10$ No
d. **$2(-2)^2 - (-2) = 10$ Yes**
e. $2(1)^2 - 8 = -6$ No

1. Since $4 \cdot 4 \cdot 4 = 64$, we know $4^3 = 64$, so $n + 2 = 3$, giving $n + 2 - 2 = 3 - 2$, $n = 1$.

2. If $8x = 2x + 3$, then $3x + 5 = $
Solve for x in the equation:
$8x = 2x + 3$
$8x - 2x = 2x - 2x + 3$
$6x = 3$
$x = \dfrac{3}{6} = \dfrac{1}{2}$

Substitute $x = \dfrac{1}{2}$ in the expression $3x + 5$:
$3 \cdot \dfrac{1}{2} + 5 = \dfrac{3}{2} + 5 = 6\dfrac{1}{2}$

In the grid, you may use 6.5 or $\dfrac{13}{2}$. (Remember, mixed numbers aren't used in PSAT grids.)

1.

2.

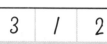

It's Prime Time!

The PSAT math sections include multiple-choice questions and grid-in questions. Topics include numbers and operations; algebra and functions; geometry and measurement; and statistics, probability, and data analysis. Math topics that most first-semester juniors have not yet covered are excluded from the test. Here is a PSAT prep problem for you to solve.

A prime number is an integer greater than 1 that is evenly divisible only by itself and 1. Which of following represents a prime number when n = 2?

a. $n^2 + 4$ b. $n^2 + 3n$ c. $7n$

d. $4n + 1$ e. $n^3 - 1$

Merit and Recognition

The PSAT is also known as the National Merit Scholarship Qualifying Test. In addition to providing firsthand practice for the SAT Reasoning Test, the PSAT also gives you a chance to enter the National Merit Scholarship Corporation (NMSC) scholarship programs.

Here are two more PSAT prep problems:

1. Which of the following binomial products is correct?

   a. $(2x + 3)(2x - 3) = 4x^2 + 9$

   b. $(2x - 3)^2 = 4x^2 - 6x + 9$

   c. $(x + 3)(x - 4) = x^2 + x - 12$

   d. $2x(x - 3) - y(x - 3) = (2x - y)(x - 3)$

   e. $(2x + 3)(x - 4) = 2x^2 - 5x + 12$

2. Which of the following lines is not parallel to the equation $y = \frac{1}{2}x - 4$?

   a. $y = \frac{1}{2}x + 1$

   b. $y = \frac{3}{6}x - 3$

   c. $2y = x - 4$

   d. $y + \frac{1}{2}x = 1$

   e. $-y = -\frac{1}{2}x$

The answer is e.

a. $n^2 + 4 = 2^2 + 4 = 4 + 4 = 8$ (composite)

b. $n^2 + 3n = 2^2 + 3 \cdot 2 = 4 + 6 = 10$ (composite)

c. $7n = 7 \cdot 2 = 14$ (composite)

d. $4n + 1 = 4 \cdot 2 + 1 = 8 + 1 = 9$ (composite)

e. $n^3 - 1 = 2^3 - 1 = 8 - 1 = 7$ (prime)

The answers are:

1. The best way to approach this problem is to verify each product using your understanding of binomial product patterns or by using the FOIL method.
    a. $(2x + 3)(2x - 3) = 4x^2 + 9$ **Incorrect**
        Should be difference of squares: $4x^2 - 9$
    b. $(2x - 3)^2 = 4x^2 - 6x + 9$ **Incorrect**
        Should be a perfect square trinomial:
        $4x^2 - 12x + 9$
    c. $(x + 3)(x - 4) = x^2 + x - 12$ **Incorrect**
        Should be: $x^2 - x - 12$
    d. $2x(x - 3) - y(x - 3) = (2x - y)(x - 3)$ **Correct**
        Factor by grouping is like working the distributive property in reverse.
    e. $(2x + 3)(x - 4) = 2x^2 - 5x + 12$ **Incorrect**
        Should be: $2x^2 - 5x - 12$

2. Once you solve for y (y-intercept form), the coefficient of x is the slope. The slope in the equation $y = \frac{1}{2}x - 4$ is $\frac{1}{2}$. Solve for y in the possible answers then compare the slopes to $\frac{1}{2}$. Parallel lines must have the same slope.

    a. $y = \frac{1}{2}x + 1$ Yes
    b. $y = \frac{3}{6}x - 3$ Yes, $\frac{3}{6} = \frac{1}{2}$
    c. $2y = x - 4$ Yes, by dividing both sides by 2 gives $y = \frac{1}{2}x - 2$.
    d. $y + \frac{1}{2}x = 1$ **No**, by subtracting $\frac{1}{2}x$ from both sides gives $y = -\frac{1}{2}x + 1$. Slope is $\frac{1}{2}$.
    e. $-y = -\frac{1}{2}x$ Yes, slope is $\frac{1}{2}$.

Unit 11 PSAT Prep

Here's a Tip!

Relax the night before the PSAT. Don't try to cram. You will be tested on the knowledge that you have obtained over the school year. Last-minute studying will only stress you out. Hang out with friends or go to a movie—anything to get your mind off of the test.

Directions: Make copies of the grids provided on the inside back cover. Write answers to these PSAT prep problems in the grids.

I.
1. Perpendicular lines have negative reciprocal slopes, i.e. $-\frac{2}{3}$ and $\frac{3}{2}$. What is the slope of the line perpendicular to $-2y = 5x + 3$?
2. Given $x = 2y - 3$, find y if $x^3 = 8$.

II. In an analogy you want to find a pair of items that has the same relationship to each other as a given pair of items. Make the best choice for each analogy.
3. Diameter is to radius as: a. addition to subtraction, b. area to circumference, c. 2x: x, d. multiply to divide
4. Binomial: Trinomial as: a. $(x + 3):(xyz +3)$, b. triangle: square, c. bicycle: tricycle, (d) $x^3 : x^2$

Unit 12 Quadratic Equations

Quadratic Equations

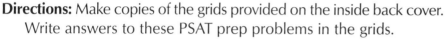

A **quadratic equation** is an equation where the highest power of x is 2, i.e. x^2. There are various methods for solving quadratic equations, including the square root method, factoring, completing the square and using the quadratic equation. Generally, quadratic equations have two solutions.

In simple quadratic equations with the variable only represented once, the square root method is probably the easiest method. Take the equation $2x^2 = 18$ as an example. To solve this, simply isolate x^2 on one side of the equation then get the square root of both sides of the equation:

Example:
$$2x^2 = 18$$
$$\frac{2x^2}{2} = \frac{18}{2}$$
$$x^2 = 9$$
$$\sqrt{x^2} = \sqrt{9}$$
$$x = 3 \text{ and } x = -3$$

Directions: Solve the following quadratic equations using the square root method:
1. $3x^2 = 12$ 2. $-4x^2 - 8 = -72$ 3. $9x^2 = 4$

Solution #97

1. If you solve for y in the equation $-2y = 5x + 3$, you will have $y = -\frac{5}{2}x - \frac{3}{2}$. The slope of the line $-\frac{5}{2}$, therefore a line perpendicular to that line would have a slope of $\frac{2}{5}$.

2. First solve $x^3 = 8$, substitute the value for x into the equation $x = 2y - 3$, then solve for y.

$$x^3 = 8 \qquad 2 = 2y - 3$$
$$x = 2 \qquad 5 = 2y$$
$$\qquad\qquad \frac{5}{2} = y$$

3. c. 2x: x, since the diameter of a circle is twice the radius.

4. Best answer is c. bicycle: tricycle, a ratio of two units (terms, wheels, etc.) to three units.

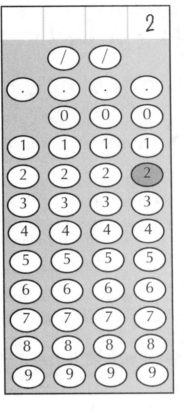

Solution #98

The answers are:

1. $3x^2 = 12$

$$\frac{3x^2}{3} = \frac{12}{3}$$
$$x^2 = 4$$
$$\sqrt{x^2} = \sqrt{4}$$
$$x = 2 \text{ and } x = -2$$

2. $-4x^2 - 8 = -72$

$$-4x^2 = -64$$
$$\frac{-4x^2}{-4} = \frac{-64}{-4}$$
$$x^2 = 16$$
$$\sqrt{x^2} = \sqrt{16}$$
$$x = 4 \text{ and } x = -4$$

3. $9x^2 = 4$

$$\frac{9x^2}{9} = \frac{4}{9}$$
$$x^2 = \frac{4}{9}$$
$$\sqrt{x^2} = \frac{\sqrt{4}}{9}$$
$$x = \frac{2}{3} \text{ and } -\frac{2}{3}$$

TLC10559 Copyright © Teaching & Learning Company, Carthage, IL 62321-0010

Factoring—Not Again!

The main reason for learning to factor polynomials is to use the skill as a tool in solving quadratic equations. First, you would write the quadratic equation in standard form. The standard form for a quadratic equation is $ax^2 + bx + c = 0$. Next, factor completely the left side of the equation. Then you can set each of the factors equal to zero and solve them separately. Finally, check your answers in the original equation. Here is an example of how it's done:

1. Write in standard form. $x^2 - 2x - 15 = 0$
2. Factor. $(x + 3)(x - 5) = 0$
3. Set factors equal to zero. $x + 3 = 0$ and $x - 5 = 0$
4. Solve. $x = -3$ and $x = 5$
5. Check your solutions. $(-3)^2 - 2(-3) - 15 = 9 + 6 - 15 = 0$
   $5^2 - 2(5) - 15 = 25 - 10 - 15 = 0$

Now, try these. Solve each quadratic equation using the factoring method.

1. $x^2 - 2x - 8 = 0$ **2.** $4x^2 = 9$ **3.** $3x^2 - 5x = 2$

The Quadratic Formula

$$x = \frac{-b \pm \sqrt{b^2 - 4ac}}{2a}$$

Shown above is the Quadratic Formula. This formula may be used to solve all quadratic equations. First, you need to put the equation in standard form: $ax^2 + bx + c = 0$. Next, substitute the values for a, b, and c into the equation, and then simplify.

For example, in the equation, $3x^2 - x - 2 = 0$, a = 3, b = -1 and c = -2.
Substitute the values into the Quadratic Formula, then simplify:

$$x = \frac{-(-1) \pm \sqrt{(-1)^2 - 4(3)(-2)}}{2(3)} = \frac{\pm 1 \sqrt{1 - (-24)}}{6}$$

$$x = \frac{1 \pm \sqrt{25}}{6} = \frac{1 \pm 5}{6}$$

$$x = \frac{1 + 5}{6} \text{ and } x = \frac{1 - 5}{6}$$

$$x = 1 \text{ and } x = -\frac{2}{3}$$

Check: $3(1)^2 - 1 - 2 = 3 - 1 - 2 = 0$

$$3(-\frac{2}{3})^2 - (-\frac{2}{3}) - 2 = 3(\frac{4}{9}) + \frac{2}{3} - 2$$

$$= \frac{4}{3} + \frac{2}{3} - \frac{6}{3} = 0$$

Now, you try this one:
$2x^2 + 5x = 3$

Solution #99

The answers are:

1. $x^2 - 2x - 8 = 0$
$(x - 4)(x + 2) = 0$
$x - 4 = 0$ and $x + 2 = 0$
$x = 4$ and $x = -2$

Check: $4^2 - 2 \cdot 4 - 8 = 16 - 8 - 8 = 0$
$(-2)^2 - 2(-2) - 8 = 4 + 4 - 8 = 0$

2. $4x^2 = 9$
$4x^2 - 9 = 0$
$(2x + 3)(2x - 3) = 0$
$2x + 3 = 0$ and $2x - 3 = 0$
$2x = -3$ $2x = 3$
$x = \dfrac{-3}{2}$ and $x = \dfrac{3}{2}$

Check: $4(-\dfrac{3}{2})^2 = 4 \cdot \dfrac{9}{4} = 9$
$4(\dfrac{3}{2})^2 = 4 \cdot \dfrac{9}{4} = 9$

3. $3x^2 - 5x = 2$
$3x^2 - 5x - 2 = 0$ (general trinomial)
$(3x^2 - 6x) + (x - 2) = 0$
$3x(x - 2) + 1(x - 2) = 0$
$(3x + 1)(x - 2) = 0$
$3x + 1 = 0$ and $x - 2 = 0$
$3x = -1$
$x = -\dfrac{1}{3}$ and $x = 2$

Check: $3(-\dfrac{1}{3})^2 - 5(-\dfrac{1}{3}) = \dfrac{3}{9} + \dfrac{5}{3} = \dfrac{6}{3} = 2$
$3(2)^2 - 5 \cdot 2 = 3 \cdot 4 - 10 = 12 - 10 = 2$

Solution #100

$$x = \frac{1}{2} \text{ and } x = -3$$

In standard form, the equation is written $2x^2 + 5x - 3 = 0$ with $a = 2$, $b = 5$ and $c = -3$.

$x = \dfrac{-5 \pm \sqrt{(5)^2 - 4(2)(-3)}}{2(2)}$

$x = \dfrac{-5 \pm \sqrt{25 + 24}}{4}$

$x = \dfrac{-5 \pm \sqrt{49}}{4}$

$x = \dfrac{-5 \pm 7}{4}$

$x = \dfrac{-5 + 7}{4}$ and $x = \dfrac{-5 - 7}{4}$

$\longrightarrow x = \dfrac{1}{2}$ and $x = -3$

Check: $2(\dfrac{1}{2})^2 + 5(\dfrac{1}{2}) - 3 = 0$

$\dfrac{2}{4} + \dfrac{5}{2} - 3 = 0$

$\dfrac{1}{2} + 2\dfrac{1}{2} - 3 = 0$

$0 = 0$

$2(-3)^2 + 5(-3) - 3 = 0$
$18 - 15 - 3 = 0$
$0 = 0$

Teaching Tips

Tip #1
Get Up for the Challenge

Congratulations on becoming an essential part of the gateway to success for many students. Not that you need anymore pressure, but did you know that algebra is a deciding "factor" in determining success for most students? There is a positive correlation between completing algebra and being college bound, highly employable, enrolled in higher math and sciences courses and confident in higher learning.

Your success and the success of your students will depend a great deal on your enthusiasm and excitement for teaching the course. So, get up for the challenge!

Your enthusiasm and excitement have to be genuine. You can't fake it—students will know right away if you are. You don't necessarily have to be the "Dick Vitale" of algebra teachers. But within your own personality, your enthusiasm and excitement must be evident and maintained through the good times and the challenges that await you, which is not always easy. It is important for you to know "what kindles your fire," "what pushes your button," "what inspires and excites you about teaching algebra." Is it the importance of the teacher's role in positively shaping and impacting students' lives and futures? Is it the excitement of planning and presenting an effective lesson, then watching the lights of knowledge and skill turn on in a young person's mind? Is it a fond memory of a great teacher that you had or another educational experience, good or bad? Is it the money (yah right)? Is it a great book or a great movie (e.g. *Stand and Deliver*, *To Sir with Love*)? Is it the desire to make a difference? Is it a combination of these things or something completely different? It is up to you to determine that.

Once you have determined the source of your inspiration, use it. Find that quiet place inside of you, through your choice of vehicle (prayer, meditation, yoga, music, nature, motivational speeches, books, etc.), and connect with this source as often as needed. Let's face it, we're all human and we must, from time to time, renew and rekindle our enthusiasm and drive. We must also keep exploring other ways to keep the teaching fires burning when other methods may be fading. In an ideal situation, all students are bright, motivated and polite with supportive parents. In such situations, teachers find it easier to display and maintain enthusiasm and excitement. But teaching is not always an ideal situation. Public education today is influenced by a myriad of variables, including societal factors (poverty, single-family households and discipline), economics, politics and culture influences. Students are not always motivated and eager to learn. Students are not always polite, well disciplined and have sound math fundamentals. However, these are the students who need an enthusiastic and motivated teacher most of all. Too often it's the teachers in the ideal settings with bright and motivated students who get the recognition when in reality it's the teachers of the less motivated, less fundamentally sound and at-risk students that generate the best teaching. If you're in one of those situations, it is not impossible. It is a challenge, but doable. You will have to dig deeper and search within yourself for the constant drive, passion and energy needed for success.

It's in there and you can find it! Just remember, you're not alone. There is a broad range of supports and resources available to you. This book will certainly help; in addition to the algebra workouts, there are subsequent tips ranging from developing lesson plans to classroom management to fostering parental involvement. Don't be alarmed by the responsibility that rests on your shoulders. Just relax, tap into your source of boundless enthusiasm and excitement for teaching algebra and you'll do just fine!

Tip #2
Lesson Planning

Preparation through lesson planning is a major key to successful teaching. Developing effective algebra lesson plans involves three levels of planning:

1. long-term lesson planning
2. grading period (quarterly or semester) planning
3. daily lesson planning

Long-Term Lesson Planning

Your algebra curriculum guides, achievement standards, course objectives and math department chairperson are the primary resources for developing a long-term lesson plan. The entire algebra course should be mapped out in terms of units for each grading period. Long-term lesson plans should encompass all algebra curricula requirements and should be developed cognizant of all state-wide and district algebra assessments. Adjustments to long-term lesson plans should be made at the end of grading periods based on instructional achievements and additional needs of your students.

Grading Period Planning

Grading period planning should be documented in a daily planner with specific objectives for the lesson. Plans should be reviewed and revised on a weekly basis, based on instructional achievements and the needs of students.

Daily Lesson Planning

The daily lesson plan is a detailed blueprint describing the essential elements and activities for the lesson. These plans should be reviewed and revised daily, based on instructional achievements and the needs of students.

Daily lesson plans should be developed on individual sheets of paper/forms and filed for future use. There are also useful computer programs for developing lesson plans. Lesson Plans for Windows® is one of the most recommended.

Effective daily plans contain the following elements:
1. **Workout:** Workouts are excellent tools for getting the algebra lesson started. Workouts may be used to introduce a lesson or randomly throughout the school year to engage students with various algebraic concepts.
2. **Objective:** The lesson's objective is a specific description of the knowledge or skill that students should learn from the lesson.
3. **Introduction:** The introduction can include several elements:
   a. introduction of the concept
   b. review of prerequisite skills
   c. an overview or demonstration of the skill
   d. a discussion of needed supplies and materials
   e. an exercise to grab students' interest and enthusiasm
4. **Instruction:** This is the core of the lesson. Methods of instruction will vary depending on the topic, student learning styles, teaching styles/methods, student skill level and needs of the students.
5. **Independent and/or Group Practice:** Give students an opportunity to try the skill individually or as part of a group activity. Follow this practice with immediate feedback. Additional instruction/demonstration and independent practice may be needed.
6. **Assessment of Lesson's Effectiveness:** Determine the effectiveness of the lesson and any remaining students' needs. Adjust your daily lesson plans if necessary. There are a number of ways to assess lesson effectiveness, including observing student work, asking questions, having students work problems on the board, short quizzes, etc.
7. **Summary/Review and Additional Practice (Homework):** At the end of the lesson, the teacher should provide a brief summary of the lesson. The lesson's objective should be reinforced through additional practice (homework, projects, special assignments).

Emergency Lesson Plans

Every teacher should maintain on file (school office or classroom) three sets of emergency lessons on file. These plans should be generic algebraically so they can be used anytime throughout the year. Helpful Tip: Videotape the lessons in advance. It's the next best thing to you being there!

Tip #3
Get Connected

Get connected to another math teacher(s), preferably someone who is teaching or has taught algebra. Whether you call the process mentoring, coaching, partnering, teaming or advising, it really doesn't matter. Research shows that all teachers—novice, experienced, veteran—benefit from such a relationship which fosters professional development.[1]

If you are a first or second year teacher, chances are you've already been placed with a mentor, someone to guide and support your progression as a teacher. Generally, in mentoring, a novice teacher is assigned to a more experienced teacher. If you have not been placed with a mentor, make a request to your content supervisor or school administrator, or seek out a mentor on your own. Most experienced and seasoned veteran teachers would appreciate the opportunity to share their knowledge and wisdom with an eager newcomer. Be careful to approach someone who you think is accepting of a novice teacher, someone who sees the beginning teacher as a developing professional, rather than as someone who needs to be "fixed."[2] A good mentor should be someone with whom you feel comfortable, someone you can ask the difficult and more practical questions, which may not have been addressed in your teacher preparation classes or in staff development activities, such as:

1. What do you do with Johnny who doesn't have the basic computational skills needed to succeed in algebra?
2. How to handle Billie who continues to be disrespectful and disruptive, despite submitting two disciplinary referrals to the assistant principal who refuses to take action.
3. What is the best way to respond to a belligerent Mrs. Bullet who blames you for her daughter's poor test scores, even though her daughter is inattentive in class and seldom completes her homework assignments?

A mentoring connection may include an array of activities such as mutual classroom observations and team teachings, and it may involve discussions of topics such as lesson planning, classroom management, lesson delivery and teaching style, discipline and parent involvement—just to name a few. Most importantly, however, the relationship should be supportive and nourishing. If you don't have an ideal "connection" with your currently assigned mentor, you may diplomatically request a change or just simply add another teacher, a more compatible match, to your network of guidance and support.

No matter their background or level of experience, it is beneficial for all teachers to maintain some kind of professional connection. Such connections can reduce attrition, anxiety and burnout, while improving the quality of teaching and the results for students.

Staying connected can take on many forms, shapes and sizes. It could be as simple as getting together once a week for lunch/discussion or as basic as regular e-mail exchanges and updates. It may be a one-on-one relationship or it may involve a group of teachers. Getting and staying connected is a win-win situation for all involved, particularly your students.

Tip #4
Early Classroom Structure

When asked for advice on being successful, an outstanding algebra teacher once said, "Don't smile for the first three months of school." Though the statement is not

[1] Danielson, C. "Mentoring beginning teachers: The case for mentoring." *Teaching and Change*, 6(3), pgs. 251-257, 1999.
[2] Rowley, J. "The good mentor." *Educational Leadership*, 56, pgs. 20-22, 1999.

meant to be taken literally, the point, however, was well taken. In establishing classroom rules and expectations, it is best to start out the year with too much structure than too little. It is far easier to ease restrictions as the school year progresses than to remedy problems caused by a weak classroom structure. Here are some suggestions for structuring your classroom:

1. Carefully plan and implement strategies that involve high expectations.
2. Establish classroom rules that are fair while promoting a classroom environment that is safe, orderly and conducive to learning.
3. Reinforce classroom rules and expectations daily. Display them clearly in your classroom.
4. Use assigned seating charts, desk labels and information cards to rapidly learn students' names, personalities and parent contact information.
5. Establish protocol for everything: entering the classroom, exiting the classroom, asking questions, getting out of seats, turning in assignments, going to the restroom, talking in class, obtaining permission, taking books and materials home, etc.
6. Clearly define and enforce consequences for misbehavior.
7. Involve parents early and let them know your rules and expectations.
8. Don't make exceptions. It sends a message of vulnerability and indecisiveness.

Establishing structure early on in the school year will make the rest of the school year more manageable and enjoyable for you and your students.

Tip #5
ABCs of Classroom Management
It has been estimated that the average teacher in an urban setting spends at least one-third of classroom time on classroom management-related issues. This takes valuable time away from actual classroom instruction. This is the number one factor that drives many teachers out of the profession. Here are some basic ABCs of classroom management:

A. **Atmosphere.** Effective classroom management involves creating an inviting atmosphere for learning, which includes a well-arranged and visually stimulating classroom, clear rules and expectations, enforced rules with definite consequences and instruction that is stimulating, exciting and applicable.

B. **Be prepared.** Preparation is key to effective classroom management. The better prepared you are, the more confident, relaxed and in control you are. Preparation not only involves developing outstanding lesson plans, it also means having a plan for dealing with distractions and disruptive students.

C. **Cooperation.** Remember that educating children is a collaborative effort, involving an entire "village" of people, like parents, administrators, counselors, peers, mentors, role models, community leaders, coaches and social workers. Helping students reach their full potential is a team endeavor. Know all the resources available to you and use them as much as possible.

Tip #6
Establishing Classroom Rules
The importance of establishing classroom rules is well-known. There are as many approaches to developing and implementing rules as there are rules themselves. Some teachers favor the idea of giving students a voice in establishing classroom rules. Others prefer to establish the rules themselves. No matter which approach you use, there are some key points you should keep in mind.

1. Classroom rules must be established from the first day of school and reinforced as frequently as possible.
2. Rules without consequences are not rules at all.
3. Classroom rules should be relevant, clear and concise. They should be displayed in the classroom.
4. Students and parents should acknowledge their understanding of the classroom rules and the consequences for not following them, you could have students and parents sign a form describing the rules and consequences and keep the signed document on file.

Classroom rules should address the following issues:
1. Respectfulness for all people and property
2. Classroom protocol
3. Expectations regarding preparedness, attendance, promptness, attentiveness, assignment completion, effort and honesty
4. Classroom disruptions and consequences for rule violations

Example of Rules Acknowledgement Form

Classroom Rules
Mrs. Smith-Jones Algebra Class

1. Students will be respectful and courteous to all people.
2. Students will be in their assigned seats, prepared for class and ready to work when the bell rings.
3. Students will obtain permission before speaking or leaving their desks.
4. Students will pay attention and always try their hardest.
5. Students will respect school property and the property of others.
6. Classroom disruptions, cheating and dishonesty will not be tolerated.
7. Assignments should be completed and turned in on time. Late and incomplete work is subject to penalty.
8. Students will obey classroom rules at all times. Consequences for not following rules include: loss of privileges, parent conferences, detention and administrative action (suspension, expulsion).

I fully understand the classroom rules presented above, and I intend to follow these rules to the best of my ability.

Student	Date
Parent	Date

Tip #7
Fundamentals: The Root of Many Problems
Nearly all successful algebra teachers will tell you that the mastery of basic computational skills is a prerequisite for success in algebra. These skills, at a minimum, include mastery of the following: 1. multiplication tables (with adequate speed and accuracy without the use of a calculator) at least for the 1s through 12s; 2. operations (addition, subtraction, multiplication and division) with fractions and decimals; 3. basic integer operations and 4. solving simple proportions. Students who have not acquired these basic computational skills are severely limited in their ability to progress in algebra. Unfortunately, a growing number of students have not developed these skills before being enrolled in an algebra course. Why? Well, there are many possible reasons, including: 1. the confusion over National Council of Teachers of Mathematics (NCTM) standards regarding memorization vs. calculator-usage for solving computational problems; 2. the push to get all students in algebra; 3. increased focus on state and local assessments; 4. the emphasis on higher level thinking skills before a knowledge base or basic skill level is attained and 5. the lack of continuous, intense drilling on the math fundamentals.

So as an algebra teacher, what can you do? First of all, you should assess your students' basic computational skills early on in the course. Administer a basic skills diagnostic exam, which contains a broad range of computational problems such as the following:

1. 209×78
2. $25\overline{)625}$
3. Compute the average: 12, 24, 48.
4. $14 - 2 \times 6$
5. $\frac{3}{4} = \frac{6}{3}$
6. $3^2 - 4$
7. $\frac{2}{3} + \frac{5}{6}$
8. $5\frac{1}{8} - \frac{3}{4}$
9. $3\frac{1}{2} \times 6$
10. $2\frac{1}{3} \div \frac{7}{9}$
11. $0.45 + 5 + 4.5$
12. $5.3 - 0.97$
13. 3.9×4.07
14. $.5\overline{)6.5}$
15. $-5 + 12$
16. $13 - 20$
17. $-6 - (-11)$
18. $-23 + -23$
19. $-6 \cdot 4$
20. $\frac{-15}{-3}$

After you administer and score the diagnostic exam, return the exams to your students, go over the results and review the problems with them. Because students' skills are sometimes temporarily weakened due to lapses in use that occur during summer or semester breaks, administer a second diagnostic exam within the first few days of the course. Use these results to make determinations about students' readiness for algebra. Notify the school counselor and the parent(s) of any student for whom you have concerns about their algebra readiness (scoring below 70%). Depending on the severity of the deficiency, suggest any or all of the following: 1. schedule change to a course that would improve their basic computational skills; 2. supplemental assistance through tutoring or educational centers and/or 3. greater parental involvement in the form of nightly drills and practice activities. If the overall average of your class is below 80% on a diagnostic inventory/assessment, it is recommended that you incorporate supplemental drills, exercises and assignments into your lesson planning. Also, on your quizzes and tests include basic computational problems to keep students' skills sharp. The time and attention spent on basic computational skills will pay big dividends throughout the course of the school year.

Tip #8
Multitask with Technology
Learn to use available technological devices/resources/tools for as many teaching components as possible, including: enhancing home/school communication, lesson planning, classroom management, instructional delivery, scoring of tests/assignments, recording grades and maintaining records. There is a broad range of technology, many of which you probably already have, that would enhance your effectiveness as an algebra teacher and make your job easier. First, let's start with the telephone (and/or cell phone). You remember that little device you hold up to your ear or talk into via a speaker. Well, the telephone is the most valuable technological teaching resource/tool ever invented and yet the most underused. Today, there is a tremendous push to put computers in every classroom and to have all schools online. However, only in recent years have policy and decision-makers began to understand the importance of having a telephone in the classroom, despite its invention practically a century ago. The camera is another wasted opportunity. Every other field/discipline or profession has utilized the camera to advance their cause. However, in education, we have failed to reap the enormous benefit of this technology. The drive for computers goes on while the importance and usefulness of the telephone and camera, which are far more valuable in the learning process particularly pertaining to classroom management, have been virtually ignored.

What follows are some examples of the technological devices/resources/tools and their potential usefulness to you as an algebra teacher, starting with the phone and camera:

- **Telephones (cell phones)** in the classroom are useful in fostering effective communication between teachers, parents and the education community. If there is not a telephone in your classroom, the solution is simple: use your personal cell phone and write-off the cost for school-related calls as a business expense.

- **Cameras** provide a number of benefits to the classroom environment, including:
  1. serving as an instructional tool to improve teaching;
  2. reducing the redundancy and repetition which has become an unnecessary part of education;
  3. maintaining a safe and orderly school environment and
  4. improving student attentiveness and accountability while reducing behavior problems and disruptions (the Mississippi pilot project has proven that).[3] Also, videotaping emergency lessons in your absence is an excellent use of the technology. It's the next best thing to having you in the classroom. The issue

[3]Tisdale, P.A. Principal, "Cameras in the Classroom," May/June 2004 Vol. 83 No. 5.

of cameras in the classrooms is one that is far more controversial and political than the use of any other available technology. However, if you feel strongly about their potential usefulness in your classroom, get permission from your principal/supervisor to use your own camera periodically for any or all of the benefits mentioned above.

- **Computers and Internet resources** are invaluable to today's algebra. Maintaining students' grades and information, communicating with parents via e-mails, lesson planning, research and preparation and reinforcing lessons and providing practice through interactive software—just to list a few of their uses. Review and bookmark a number of Web sites and excellent resources and tools for teaching algebra. There are many Web sites available to assist algebra teachers. Here are a just few to get you started:
  http://www.learner.org/index.html#
  http://www.mathsslideshow.com/Alg1/previews.htm
  http://www.webmath.com/index4.html
- **PowerPoint** is an ideal presentational vehicle for algebra lessons, particularly for showing steps in solving equations, presenting algebraic concepts and principles, displaying graphs and instructional graphics and demonstrating problem-solving strategies. PowerPoint helps create algebra lessons that flow and bring excitement to every lesson, while providing teachers more freedom to interact with their students and move about the classroom to assist students.
- **Graphing calculators** should be used on occasion to reinforce ideas/concepts already presented in the classroom, in particular: graphing linear equations and inequalities, solving systems of equations and graphing solutions to quadratic equations.
- **Online grade books** are wonderful technological tools for enhancing parent/teacher communication, for getting parents more actively involved in their children's progress and for motivating students. Online grade books allow teachers to spend less time on administrative tasks and provide secure and private records of students' attendance, test/quiz scores and completed assignments.
- **Scantron grading machines** and test grading technology should be used to administer short and frequent quizzes to maintain students' algebraic skills and to provide instantaneous feedback on the areas of students' strengths as well as areas that need additional review.

Tip #9
Use Short Frequent Quizzes
One of the best ways to develop, improve and sustain students' basic algebraic skills is to give short, frequent quizzes. These quizzes should range from three to eight problems and should be able to be completed in a short amount of time. Give feedback and review the solutions as soon as possible—no later than the next class meeting.

Scantron grading machines using multiple-choice Scantron grade sheets make these quizzes easy for teachers. Scantron grading machines can be set to provide instant feedback on the areas of students' strengths and weaknesses. If your math department or school does not use this equipment, work with other teachers, administrators and parents to obtain it. If you do not have the equipment, you can also have fellow students grade papers or each student grade their own.

Chart student progress on the quizzes. The quiz grades should be weighed at a level that does not elicit test/quiz anxiety, but makes the quizzes significant enough so that students will be encouraged to do their best. Quizzes should include cumulative items from previous units, areas that need improvement and skills from current units. You will be amazed by the effectiveness of this technique in building and maintaining student skill levels and in building student confidence.

Below are two examples of the type of short quizzes that carry a big punch:

Sample Quiz A

Solve for the variable. (Show all necessary steps.)
1. $-x = -\frac{1}{2}$
2. $-3x - 8 = 19$
3. $\frac{3x}{2} + 4 = 13$
4. $6 - 2x = 5(x + 4)$
5. Review: Find the average: -30, 18, -3, -5, 15

Sample Quiz B

Factor:
1. $x^2 - 36$
2. $x^2 + 5x + 30$
3. $25x^2 - 40x + 16$
4. $2x^2 - 5x - 3$

Tip #10
Fostering Parental Involvement
Effective and consistent school-home communication is a critical component of student success and achievement in algebra and in school overall. Research shows that parental involvement has a positive affect on students' attitudes toward school and toward particular subject areas. Parental involvement improves students' classroom behavior, time spent on homework, expectation for the future, absenteeism, motivation and retention.[4] Your school district and school may already have strategies in place to promote parental involvement. However, here are a few tips that you can use at the classroom level to foster greater parental involvement:

1. Make telephone calls to parents periodically. Know their work phone numbers, home phone numbers, cell phone numbers, physical addresses and their e-mail addresses. Phone calls that provide updates on student successes and the areas where they need improvement will be appreciated by parents.
2. Have parents sign and return as many tests, quizzes and assignments as possible. Periodically send home individualized notes, greetings and notices to parents.
3. Utilize current technology, including e-mailing, school/district Web site and an online grade book. If your school or district has a Web site, use it. If not, work with others in your school and community to develop one. There are also Web sites like www.ineteacher.com that can assist you. Make yourself available to parents and students through e-mails. Use an online grade book, such as mygradebook.com to keep parents abreast of as much as possible: grades, unexcused absences, missing assignments, behavioral concerns, upcoming assignments, exams and events.
4. Make your classroom inviting and celebrate parent participation. Encourage parents to participate by having special lessons, field trips, presentations and activities that include them.
5. Schedule periodic parent-teacher conferences at school. Look at these conferences as an opportunity for you and the parents to work as a team to help the student.

Make parents aware of how involvement can benefit their children. Parental involvement is the most valuable resource in helping students to succeed in their future careers.

Tip #11
Using Online Grade Books
A revolution is taking place with teachers' grade books, and its potential influence is unlimited. We are talking about the online grade book. This technology is highly recommended for you—the algebra teacher. It is certainly the wave of the future, and it has already made positive impacts over the last few years. The online grade book is transforming education. It is closing the home/school communication gap significantly, while motivating and inspiring students to do better and to be more accountable and allowing parents to be more active in the achievements/progress of their children, particularly those at the middle school and high school levels.

There are a growing number of online grade books available to teachers, schools and districts, including Grade Book Wizard and Pearson's My Grade Book, which is probably the most popular tool used today. Perhaps your school and district has already selected a vendor. If not, you may do so rather inexpensively on your own or with a group of teachers at a significant discount.

Here are just a few of the many benefits of using an online grade book:
- Allows teachers to spend less time on administrative tasks
- Provides secure and private, up-to-date, records of students' attendance, test scores and completed assignments
- Allows parents to stay more informed about their children's progress
- Motivates students to be more accountable
- Enhances home/school communication

Online grade books are user-friendly. Teachers can tailor their grading systems and policies to their preferences and customize grade tracking and reporting for each of their math classes. In addition, teachers may use their class Web site to post individual student grades, teacher comments related to an individual student, upcoming test/quiz dates, assignments, instructions, grades, announcements and policies, class calendar and handouts for students and parents, etc. Although students, parents and teachers can access the resource from any PC or Mac with Internet access, online grade books are committed to protecting the privacy of your personal and student information (through secured log-ins and the use of password technology).

Although the potential benefits of the online grade book are tremendous, the success of the technology depends a great deal on the extent of your commitment. It is important to keep records up-to-date and to be proactive in communicating with parents and students. This technology can be an invaluable resource as you strive for teaching excellence and in helping your algebra students achieve success.

Tip #12
At-Risk and Special Education Students
Algebra provides unique opportunities and opens academic doors for a vast number of students with diverse backgrounds and unique abilities. One of the greatest joys of teaching algebra is helping students achieve success, when success might not have occurred in other courses. All students are capable of achievement in algebra, provided they enter the course with the necessary computational skills. All students are unique, with unique personalities and characteristics. They come from diverse cultural, social and economic backgrounds and have individual learning styles, motivations and goals. Your challenge, as an algebra teacher, is to provide all students with the best opportunity of succeeding in your classroom. At-risk and special education students may be among your greatest challenges as an algebra teacher, but their achievement may bring you the greatest satisfaction.

Special Education Students
There are certain students with special challenges that have to be addressed in order for them to have the same opportunities to succeed in school. These students are our special education students. By the reauthorization of the Individuals with Disabilities Act (IDEA) in 2004, all special education students should have an Individualized Education Program (IEP), designed to meet their unique needs.

[4]Cotton, K., and Wikelund, K.R. "Parent Involvement in Education." NW Regional Educational Laboratory, *http://www.nwrel.org/scpd/ sirs/3/cu6.html*, May, 1989.

As a regular classroom teacher, you are required by law to implement the IEPs of your special education students. The following tips will help you:
1. Know which students have IEPs.
2. Read each IEP thoroughly.
3. Insert a summary of each student's modifications and accommodations in your planning book.
4. When recommended by the IEP team, allow students to use all assistive technology (calculators, computers, etc.).
5. Participate in IEP meetings at every opportunity.
6. Incorporate the needs of special needs students in your lesson plans.
7. Work closely with your special education teacher(s) and involve the parents.

More likely than not, at least one or more of your students has a disability that falls in the category of emotional disturbance (ED). There is a movement among educational professionals to emphasize the term behaviorally disordered, which is believed to be a less stigmatizing label than emotional disturbance found in IDEA. These students exhibit a broad range of behaviors that may impede their educational performance (and the performance of other students).

There is a great deal of research and instructional strategies on teaching ED students available, including Positive Behavioral Supports (PBS), methods of modifying teaching styles and expectations, and ways of tolerating negative behaviors. Here are some practical tips to help you meet this growing challenge in public education:
1. Involve the parents, administrators, counselors and other support staff (special education resource teachers, school psychologist, school social worker) as much as possible. Participate in student IEP meetings. Articulate your concerns and develop strategies and support that will best serve the students.
2. Insist that ED students abide by the same classroom rules as other students. Do not allow them to take control of your classroom. If other students observe disruptive behaviors, it will undermine your authority as a teacher and your ability to maintain a safe and orderly learning environment.
3. For students who are not responsive or persistently disruptive, request a special education resource teacher be with you in the classroom. The student is required to have one if recommended by the IEP team. The special education resource teacher can remove the students temporarily to an alternate setting when he or she is too disruptive.
4. Incorporate proven strategies:
   a. behavior contracts
   b. positive reinforcements
   c. time-outs
   d. traditional consequences for misbehavior
5. Maintain your self-control at all times. Don't belittle or embarrass the students. Don't get in a power struggle with them; don't let them get away with being disobedient.

At-Risk Students
At-risk students are at a greater risk of failure and/or dropping out of school than other students. Socio-economic factors often have the greatest impact in this determination. Many of these students come from poor neighborhoods and have minimal parental support and involvement in their education. Arguably, teaching at-risk students is the most demanding and challenging assignment in the teaching profession. If you have at-risk students, here are some practical tips to help you:
1. Create a classroom culture that promotes success. Map out a course for students to achieve success and show them how to navigate it. At-risk students need to believe that
   a. success is achievable
   b. they control their own success and future
   c. their efforts and commitment will be rewarded
   d. that you believe that they will succeed

The best way to establish a classroom culture/climate that is nurturing and supportive is by positively addressing your students. As a teacher, you have to sell them on themselves and your belief that success is attainable for each of them. Reinforce this at every opportunity.
2. Remain supportive and maintain discipline. Sometimes being supportive and nurturing has become synonymous with being lax and weak. When dealing with at-risk students, you need to implement even greater structure, rely more on your classroom management skills and apply greater discipline with firm consequences for misbehavior. However, you must emphasize to your students that your demands and expectations are part of the formula for their success.
3. Turn basic skill development into activities that are meaningful and engaging. Too often, at-risk students are tracked into substandard courses with low expectations. Though such courses provide an adequate review of basic math skills, the courses do little to inspire students. Current research suggests at-risk students should be involved in learning that is meaningful and engaging. As a teacher of at-risk students, you must be creative in your efforts. Discover ways of implementing algebraic concepts into activities that are practical, meaningful and engaging.
4. Involve the parents. Don't assume that parents of at-risk students don't want to be involved. Most parents do want to be involved in their child's education. They are looking for ways to be involved. Be persistent in seeking parental involvement. If your first few efforts are unsuccessful, keep trying. Your next effort could be the one that makes the difference.
5. Implement a tutoring program. If at all possible, implement a tutoring program, before or after school for one hour each week. Often, at-risk students will respond better in small groups or in one-on-one settings. A tutoring program is an excellent way to provide students with extra help, to mentor and counsel students and foster healthy student-teacher relationships.
6. Reply on available support. Use support personnel and support systems available to you. Involve school administrators, program coordinators, counselors, mentors, parole officers, parents and other support staff. Finally, organizations like Big Brother/Big Sister, 100 Black Men and other volunteer organizations within your educational community can be useful.

Tip #13
Use of the Graphing Calculator
The successful use of graphing calculators in teaching calculus students has spurred a movement for the use of technology in algebra and other math courses. Because the elements of teaching algebra have developed independently of the graphing calculator, it is only appropriate to question the effectiveness of technology in the achievement of algebra students, particularly in middle and high schools. Research and views on the effectiveness of using graphing calculators in teaching algebra, particular at the secondary level, are mixed. Most research has indicated that the graphing calculator has had a positive impact on student achievement.[5] The National Council of Teachers of Mathematics has gone as far as recommending the use of graphing calculator technology in achieving national standards in mathematics.[6] Other research and opinions may differ significantly. There are some educators who believe that the use of technology can, not only, confuse students, but also mask their lack of conceptual understanding and computational weaknesses. Even supporters of the use of graphing calculators generally agree that the technology should not replace the learning of algebraic skills/concepts, but rather supplement the algebra curriculum, providing further understanding and encourage further exploration. Obviously, more research is needed. But for now, here's a recommendation for you, provided that is is consistent with your school district's algebra curriculum/policies: In teaching Algebra I, at secondary level, the primary purpose for using graphing calculators

should simply be to provide students with exposure and enhance their awareness of the technology. By no means should you require Algebra I students to purchase a graphing calculator. If your school is fortunate enough to own a classroom set, fine! If so, use the graphing calculator periodically to reinforce ideas/concepts already presented in the classroom, in particular: graphing linear equations and inequalities, solving systems of equations and graphing solutions to quadratic equations.

As an algebra teacher, by all means, you should own and use a graphing calculator on occasion in your lessons. There are a number of excellent models for algebra, including the most popular Texas Instruments TI-83 and TI-84. Use can find a used graphing calculator at a reasonable price, and they make a great tax deduction for teachers. Ideally, when demonstrating the use of the graphing calculator, you would like to project the calculator's display on your overhead projector screen, provided that you have the equipment to do so. If not, hopefully you have a classroom set of calculators that students may use to follow along with you. When using only one calculator, without any equipment to project the display, just do the best you can! Pass the calculator around the classroom and allow as many students as possible to view and participate in the demonstration.

To enhance your understanding and skills with the graphing calculator, there are a number of resources available. Product manuals are useful as well as the manufacturer Web sites and technical assistance lines. Unfortunately, teacher education programs continue to lag behind, particularly in the implementation of technology to enhance the teaching of mathematics. Here are a few of many resources that are available to you:
1. Texas Instruments: Topics in Algebra
   http://education.ti.com/downloads/guidebooks/apps/83topics_in_algebra/alg1-book.pdf
2. Video Math Tutor
   http://www.livevideo.com/video/VideoMathTutor/25A4C3F0FD2E449282C8C6DD0D7BF700/how-to-really-use-the-ti-84-gr.aspx
3. Cool math's online graphing calculator
   http://www.coolmath.com/graphit/index.html

Feel at ease when you share and explore the technology with your algebra students.

Tip #14
Be Your Own Resource!
A major key to becoming a successful algebra teacher is to stockpile an arsenal of reference materials, lesson plans, assessment instruments (test and quizzes) and notes detailing proven approaches/strategies. In other words, become your own resource. Following are ways you can successfully accomplish this:
1. Organize and maintain files. Include lesson plans that you have developed and ones that you discovered that are successful and appealing. You should keep at least one copy of all the versions of tests and quizzes on file. Include in the files curriculum guides, articles, tips and notes from your teaching experiences. Also maintain a file of telephone numbers and addresses of people and organizations that can be helpful to you as a teacher.
2. Maintain a personal library of textbooks, reference books and educational videos and DVDs. From time to time, videotape your own lessons and save them in your personal library.
3. Develop and store your own math workouts. When you think of an interesting problem or see an intriguing algebraic idea, write it down and save it.
4. Bookmark useful Web sites.
5. Do your own research and keep notes on effective teaching methods and strategies.
6. Do your reading. On the nightstand, always have one fun book and one book related to the profession of teaching

[5]Smith, K.B., and Shotsberger, P.G. "Assessing the use of graphing calculators in college algebra: reflecting on dimensions of teaching and learning." *School Science and Mathematics,* 97(7), pgs. 368-373, 199?
[6]National Council of Teachers of Mathematics, 2000.